The Effective Trustee

Getting the Work Done

by Kevin Ford

The Effective Trustee

Part One: Roles and Responsibilities
Part Two: Aims and Resources
Part Three: Getting the Work Done

A DIRECTORY OF SOCIAL CHANGE PUBLICATION

THE EFFECTIVE TRUSTEE
Part Three:
Getting the Work Done

A practical guide for charity trustees and members of management committees of voluntary organisations

by Kevin Ford

Published by the **Directory of Social Change**
Radius Works, Back Lane, London, NW3 1HL, 071-435 8171.

Designed and typeset by Tony Goodman

© Directory of Social Change 1994
The Directory of Social Change is an educational charity.
Registration No 800517

Printed and bound in Britain. ISBN 1-873860-25-0

Kevin Ford

Kevin Ford is an independent consultant who has specialised in work with voluntary and charitable organisations. He has worked with a large number of managing committees on issues ranging from induction, roles and responsibilities, effective working practices to resolving conflict. In 1991/92 he completed research on the training needs of charity trustees for the Charity Commissioners and NCVO. He lives in Leicester and is himself a trustee.

Acknowledgements

My thanks to **Michael Norton** for his patient editing of the whole *"Effective Trustee"* series, and to **Yvonne Quinn** for word-processing all the drafts.

This book has been produced with generous support from Barclays Bank PLC. The book has been published by the Directory of Social Change. Barclays Bank PLC does not necessarily share the views expressed nor do they accept responsibility for the accuracy of the information or for any expenses or losses caused as a result thereof.

Barclays Bank has a substantial and wide-ranging programme of community support which focuses on charitable donations and sponsorships, secondment of staff, employment initiatives as well as support for environmental projects and the arts.

Barclays believes the most effective way of channelling its charitable support is to target the specific needs of those who are young, elderly, disabled or disadvantaged. Other priority areas for charitable support are medical research and education.

Readers should consult their professional advisers if they deem this to be necessary before entering into any legal commitments.

Contents

About this book

A practical handbook

Our aim in writing this handbook is to help you in your work as a trustee or managing committee member. This book covers the main things you need to do to enable your organisation to carry out its work to best effect. It explains how to organise livelier and more effective meetings of the trustees; how to recruit the staff and volunteers you need to do the work and how to manage them. It also looks at running your organisation's premises effectively and how to solve common problems faced by trustees. It provides clear, up to date information and ideas for good practice.

Your role as a managing committee member falls into two parts: you have a legal responsibility to see that those who carry out the work of your organisation act and are treated properly and within the law. We describe this as your **trustee responsibilities**. You also have a **management responsibility** for ensuring that your staff and volunteers work efficiently and effectively to achieve progress towards your organisation's objects. Throughout this book we draw your attention to these two aspects of your role.

The handbook includes a variety of checklists and activities to make it as easy as possible to put ideas in to practice. Each chapter ends with a short self-assessment exercise.

Use of terms

A wide variety of terms are used for members of managing committees. We use the term *"trustee"* when we describe matters of trustee responsibility, otherwise we simply call members of managing committees *"committee members"*, as this is the most universal term for them.

Part of a series

"Getting the Work Done" is the third in a series of three Effective Trustee handbooks from the Directory of Social Change. Some topics mentioned in this book are covered in greater depth in the other two titles: *"Roles and Responsibilities"* and *"Aims and Resources"*. Details of their contents are given on the next page.

The series does not aim to be comprehensive. Suggestions for further reading are provided at appropriate points for those who wish to explore the ideas in greater depth. These take the form of a reference to a book number, such as: *(Book 4)*, which can be found in the booklist in *Chapter 10*, where there is also a list of useful addresses.

Who is it for?

If you are involved as a member of the **managing committee** of a charity, voluntary organisation or community group, or are thinking of getting involved, this handbook is for you.

What's in this book for you?

Reading this handbook will help you to identify what steps your committee needs to take to ensure that your staff and volunteers are well managed. You will know what to do to see that your premises are suitable for achieving your aims. You will have a clear framework to tackle common problems that arise as

The Effective Trustee Series:
Main contents of Parts 1 and 3

The Effective Trustee Part 1
Roles and Responsibilities

1. The legal structures and charitable status of your organisation.

2. The role of your organisation.

3. The role of your managing committee.
    The difference between management and trusteeship.

4. The roles and responsibilities of trustees and managing committee members.

5. Special roles: Officers and Representatives.

6. Recruiting new trustees.

7. Effective committees and ideal trustees.

The Effective Trustee Part 2
Aims and Resources

1. Planning what you do.

2. Accounting for your organisation.

3. Managing your finances.

4. Managing your assets.

5. Fundraising.

your organisation tackles its work. Lastly, you will be able to identify ways to make sure that you get the most from your involvement as a trustee.

All this will help your staff and volunteers to carry out your organisation's work even better, providing more or better quality services and achieving more of your objectives. One result for you will be a greater sense of satisfaction and purpose in your work with the organisation. You will be a more effective trustee.

Organising your meetings

NEED TO KNOW

Your responsibilities

The managing committee is responsible for making sure that its members work together effectively. This means planning and organising the work of the committee so that its members are able to complete it within the time they have available.

Your **TRUSTEE** responsibilities are to make sure that:

- The committee members *work together* to carry out all the duties for which they are responsible.
- The committee is *kept up to strength* in numbers, as set out in the governing instrument.
- Proper *records* of meetings are kept.
- The committee *meets* for at least the minimum number of times each year required in the governing instrument.
- Members of the committee are *appointed* in line with the requirements of the governing instrument.

Your **MANAGEMENT** responsibilities are to see that:

- The *purpose* of each meeting is clear.
- The *committee business* is completed effectively.
- Committee meetings are *planned in an annual cycle* to take account of regular tasks.
- All the members of the committee are able to *participate fully* in meetings.
- Decisions made in meetings are *communicated effectively* to the staff and volunteers who will implement them.
- The *skills of the committee members* are used to best effect.

Why hold meetings?

The managing committee is required to meet by the governing instrument of the organisation. There is more to the meetings than this. There are at least ten other main reasons:

- To **decide the policy** and the **strategy** of the organisation.
- To agree the **objectives, priorities and plans.**

- To receive **information** on the work, such as reports, plans, budgets, management accounts in order to **monitor progress.**

- To **evaluate the progress** and check that it is **in line with the objects** set out in the governing instrument and with the policies and priorities.

- To **solve problems** relevant to the managing committee.

- To **make decisions** on what needs to be done and who should do it.
- To **ratify** decisions that have been made elsewhere.
- To **share views** and **opinions** on issues.
- To **educate** members on the work of the organisation or issues that affect it.
- To provide **support** and social contact between members.

Make sure that all the committee members are aware of the purpose of each part of the meeting. Do not assume that they all know. If you do not do this, you can easily end up with confused expectations. This can lead to vague ineffective meetings, causing frustration and de-motivation. For more on meetings in voluntary organisations see *Book 1* in *Chapter 10*.

Working as a team

A managing committee is a team with various tasks to carry out. Successful committee meetings have three different requirements:

- Ensuring that the **tasks get done**.
- Seeing that members of the committee **work together** as a team.
- Seeing that **personal needs** of the committee members are fulfilled.

Most managing committees are geared towards getting through the business on the agenda and completing their tasks. There is little time for anything else. Yet it is important that members get to know each other, establish trust and rapport, and work well as a team. This can be achieved by:

- Allowing time for **review** of what has happened during the meeting, at the end of each meeting.
- Allowing time for **informal contact** over tea, or refreshments before or after the meeting.

- Providing **lunch or supper** to members before or after the committee meeting.
- Holding a **break** in the middle of the meeting to allow informal contacts.
- Holding **induction sessions** for new members of the committee.
- Holding special, **less formal meetings** for committee members, for example, to hear about or visit one of your projects.

Fulfilling members' needs

Managing committees seldom have time to deal with individual needs during meetings. However it is important that the committee makes it possible for its members to learn the skills, gain relevant knowledge and develop the confidence to participate effectively. Usually this development of individual members will need to take place outside regular committee meetings. It can occur through:

- An **induction process** for new members.
- Attendance on relevant **training courses**.
- **Linking** a new member to a more experienced member who can act as a mentor.
- Conducting a **skills audit** of committee members, sharing the results and using this to develop a learning programme for the committee.

Clear expectations

The committee will work most effectively when all its members are clear about the purpose and style of the managing committee meetings. If most of the team building and personal development takes place outside the formal meetings, this should be made clear. The example on page 8 describes the measures taken by one managing committee.

Example: How to improve the committee

A local organisation had a managing committee of 24 people. It met four times each year, for three hours. The organisation employed 35 staff and had a turnover of £400,000.

The agenda of each committee meeting was very packed. There was no time for anything other than business. Meetings were formal, dull, but quite efficient, in that they got through the agenda. Some members rarely contributed anything. Members complained that they did not know each other, did not understand enough about the work that was going on, did not fully understand their role, and felt intimidated by the speed at which the committee worked.

The organisation took the following steps to improve things:

- Set up sub-committees to deal with many of the day-to-day matters which otherwise found their way on to the agenda.
- Delegated more to staff and to working groups.
- Encouraged managing committee members to serve on sub-committees or groups that used their particular interests or skills.
- Held an annual induction day for committee members. This included: half a day in which staff made presentations about their work and met the committee; a session to introduce all the committee members to each other; and a session on the role and responsibilities of the committee.
- Set up a managing committee members' handbook, which included information on the background, skills and experience, and a photograph of each member.
- Made it clear that the managing committee meetings themselves were formal and might be a trifle dull, but they were necessarily so.
- Encouraged contact between committee members and staff through open days, presentations and discussions.
- Set aside a special meeting each year to review the working of the committee structure itself and make improvements.

For more on team working see *Books 5 and 8* in *Chapter 10.*

Frequency of meetings

The managing committee is obliged by the governing instrument to meet a certain number of times each year. Make sure you know how often. However, holding meetings simply because meetings must be held is poor practice and can waste everyone's time. You must have an agenda.

The agenda

The main tool for organising your meetings is the **agenda**. The agenda sets out a plan for the meeting. It is much more than just a list of headings. For each item on the agenda it should tell managing committee members exactly what will be discussed and for what purpose. The agenda enables each trustee to prepare properly for the meeting.

You are entitled to demand a proper agenda for your meetings. Don't put up with vague lists. They lead to vague meetings.

A properly planned agenda also helps the chair to control the meetings and to make sure everyone is able to contribute to discussions.

The agenda also serves as a checklist of the papers the trustees will need to read *before* the meeting. It helps trustees to keep a clear idea of why they are reading each paper.

As a general rule, managing committee meetings should confine themselves to items on the agenda. This will help trustees to prepare for the meetings. The rule should be broken only for real crises or unforeseen circumstances. It is difficult for the committee to be effective if it conducts most of its business on the hoof.

Make use of the agenda

The agenda is essential, otherwise participants will be confused or unaware about the purpose of the meeting, what is to be discussed, what results are wanted, and so on.

Setting the agenda

Your managing committee should have a procedure for putting items on the agenda. This usually involves sending items to the Chair or Secretary in advance of the meeting.

The agenda should be sent out in advance of the meeting to give time for preparation and remind committee members of the meeting.

Structuring the agenda

Someone, usually the Chair, should look over the agenda items and plan a logical order, allowing time for each item.

- Important items should be tackled early.
- Short information items can be used to warm up a meeting and to provide "breathers" between longer discussions.

Each agenda item should have

TECHNICAL DETAIL

- A title
- A description of why it is on the agenda for example:

    to give information.

    to be discussed, but not for decision.

    to solve a problem.

    to decide upon a course of action.

    to report back on action agreed previously.

    to ratify decisions delegated to sub-committees or staff.

- Accompanying papers giving relevant information (where appropriate).
- A note of who will present the agenda item.

For example, the **Director's Report** might appear as follows:

Item 6 The Director's Report.
To receive the report.
Discussion only on matters
affecting the overall purpose
of the charity.
(Paper 4: For information.)
(Director)

Avoid using agendas which are just a list of single words.

Using the agenda

To make sure that the you are clear about each item on the agenda ask yourself the following questions:

1. Why is this item on the agenda? What result do we want to achieve from considering it?

2. If the item is not appropriate for discussion at the managing committee, where should it be dealt with?

3. Is the item for:
   discussion?
       to explore views and opinions
   decision?
       to agree a course of action
   ratification?
       to confirm a recommendation
       from elsewhere
   review?
       to review progress
   information?
       without the need for discussion

4. Who will be responsible for any action agreed?

PRACTICAL POINTER

Keeping to time

A well structured agenda helps the committee to keep a clear focus on why each item is being discussed. This helps the Chair to keep order and prevent the committee falling into time traps such as:

- **Nit-picking**

  Discussing matters of detail which would be better discussed elsewhere (by staff, sub-committees or working parties)

- **Pie in the sky**

  Discussion of broad issues such as social policy or values when it is not relevant to the decision that must be made.

- **Repetition**

  Unnecessary re-discussion of the arguments which have already been thrashed out in a sub-committee and a decision recommended. Or repeating points made earlier in a discussion.

- **Rambling**

  Allowing discussion to ramble on and on, long after it has served any useful purpose.

- **Droning on**

  Endless information about a matter where a short summary will do. Can easily happen where reports are given for no real purpose.

- **Waking up**

  Having to repeat significant points because a member was not listening or had fallen asleep.

Develop a cycle of meetings

The business of the managing committee follows a cycle which repeats each year. It usually begins and ends with the Annual General Meeting (AGM) and includes planning, budgeting, monitoring and review, *as shown in the diagram below.*

Link your meetings to funding dates

Most organisations which receive money from central or local government will need to link their annual cycle to:

- The dates of deadlines for major funding applications to be submitted.
- The financial year for government (April to March).

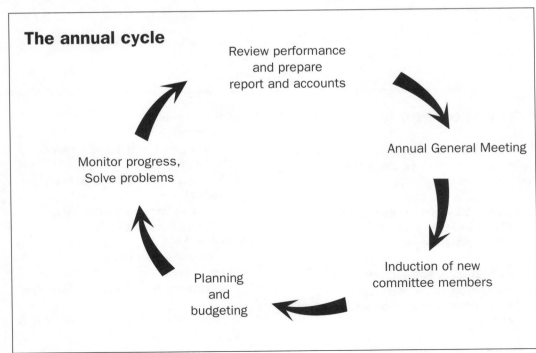

The annual cycle

Review performance and prepare report and accounts

Annual General Meeting

Induction of new committee members

Planning and budgeting

Monitor progress, Solve problems

For organisations whose financial year runs from 1st April to 31st March, this means drafting the organisation's budget in the summer, and submitting the agreed budget with the grant application to funders in the autumn (usually October or November). Final decisions from government funders are usually made between January and March for work which starts in April.

With the relevant dates in mind, it is possible to map out a typical annual calendar for a managing committee. This may vary between organisations, but all organisations have to review work, set plans and budgets, and monitor progress. For more on this see *Book 1* in *Chapter 10*.

Committee structures

Every voluntary organisation must have a **managing committee** which is ultimately responsible for its affairs. This may be called a **Board of Trustees**, a **Management Committee**, an **Executive Committee**, or other titles such as a **Council of Management.**

How big should the committee be?

The size and composition of the managing committee is set out in the governing instrument of the organisation. This will also tell you how to appoint the officers (Chair, Treasurer, Secretary).

The most effective size for a working group is generally reported to be between five and nine people. Committees become more formal and impersonal as their size increases. The laws of arithmetic dictate that each person gets far less time to contribute as the group gets larger (in a committee of twenty people, if everyone has equal time to speak, each person gets just three minutes in every hour to make

CHECK POINT

Purpose of meetings

For each item on the agenda check:

- Should we be discussing this at all?
  If not, who will discuss it?
- Why are we discussing this?
  How does it help us to carry out our role as a managing committee?
- Is it clear whether the item is for decision/information/ratification/education?
- How important is the item on the agenda?
  How long should the discussion last?
- Who is presenting the item?
- Are there relevant papers to support the discussion?
- Who will take action (if required) as a result of the discussion?

For your meetings check:

- Do some meetings have a particular focus?
- Are others more general and regular?
- Is there an annual cycle for your meetings?
- Where does each meeting fit in to the annual cycle?

For more on meetings see *Books 3 and 4* in *Chapter 10*.

their points). If you can, avoid setting up large committees. Once the number rises much above twenty people, you may struggle to have lively or effective meetings.

Sub-committees

The managing committee of a small organisation is usually able to carry out most of the business itself and does not need to delegate work to sub-committees. As an organisation becomes more complex, it may be necessary to set up sub-committees and working groups to deal effectively with the work load.

Sub-committees are small committees which are set up by the managing committee and have delegated powers to carry out a particular role. The power to set up sub-committees is usually given in the governing instrument of your organisation. Sub-committees must report back to the managing committee, to which they are fully accountable. They are usually set up to be ongoing, rather than run for a limited time. Sub-committees are usually **permanent** – and are part of the formal structure of the organisation. The chair of each sub-committee is usually a trustee and therefore sits on the main managing committee. This ensures clear lines of communication.

The main advantage of sub-committees are that they:

- Are focused on a small range of tasks.
- Can recruit members with special expertise or experience.
- Are small and can be less formal.
- Can involve staff members relevant to their work.

The main disadvantages with sub-committees tend to be:

- Communication between them and the managing committee can break down.
- They can be seen as powerful cliques – the place where real decisions are made before rubber stamping by the managing committee.
- They require even more time from managing committee members.
- Their roles may not be clearly defined, and can overlap, causing duplication and confusion.
- They may cease to have a valid purpose, but continue to meet.

TECHNICAL DETAIL

Examples of sub-committees include:

- Finance committee – to oversee the financial affairs of the organisation.
- Finance and General Purposes committee – oversees financial, general staffing and management matters.
- Executive committee – oversees general management matters.
- Investment committee – oversees the management of investments.
- Fundraising committee.
- Press and Public Relations committee.
- Employment committee.
- Project sub-committees which oversee the work of a particular project or development.

Sub-committees should have clear **terms of reference,** which spell out:

- The purpose of the sub-committee.
- The powers of action delegated to them.
- How they should report back to the managing committee.
- The composition of the committee.
- The method of appointment of members.
- The frequency of meetings.
- The role of the Chair and note taker in meetings.
- Who convenes the meetings.

- Project sub-committees may wish to become fully independent (or think they already are!). This can sometimes be a positive development.

Working groups

Working groups are less formal than sub-committees. They are set up to deal with a particular task or issue. They have a limited life and finish when they have completed their work.

Working groups should have a clear brief, much like that of a sub-committee. Members are usually selected because of interest or expertise in the task or issue to be tackled. Working groups provide a very effective forum for staff, volunteers and trustees to work together.

Examples of some issues that working groups might tackle include:

- New premises – to draw up proposals for new premises.
- Anti-racism – to develop a plan to tackle racism in the organisation.

- Management development – to investigate the structures and recommend changes.
- Children's Act – to explore the implications of new legislation on the organisation.

Provide a clear brief

People need to know exactly what they are expected to do when they join a sub-committee or working group. Only then can they decide whether they have the time, interest and expertise to make a worthwhile contribution. Some organisations go as far as writing a short job-description for sub-committee members.

It makes no sense for committee members to take on commitments which are unrealistic. All that happens is you cannot do the work properly and end up feeling guilty and frustrated. This can be avoided if you have been told clearly what is expected of you before you start.

Sub-committees and working groups

CHECK POINT

- What is the group aiming to achieve?
  What results are wanted?

- What powers does the group have? Can it make decisions?
  Do decisions need to be ratified by the managing committee?
  What are the limits to its powers?

- Who are the members? How are they appointed?
  For what reasons are people asked to join the group?

- Who convenes the group? Who chairs the meetings?

- Who takes the notes? Who receives copies?

- How does the group communicate with the managing committee and the rest of the organisation?

- How often does the group meet?

- Does the group have a limited life-span, or is it permanent?

Participation of staff in the managing committee

The paid employees of a charity are not allowed, under charity law, to be **voting members** of its managing committee. Staff may participate in meetings as observers. It is helpful to involve staff members in the committee, for two reasons:

- It builds closer contact between committee and staff.
- It enhances communication in both directions.

In small organisations with only one or two members of staff, it may be sensible for all members of staff to attend managing committee meetings. This speeds up the information flow and helps to build the sense of working together.

As the staff team gets larger, it becomes impractical and ineffective to involve them all in the managing committee. The more people who sit around the table, the less easy it is to conduct lively and effective meetings. Also, involving the whole staff team can lead to confusion about each person's role at the committee meetings. Why is each person present? Is it a good use of time? How does it affect the role of the senior staff member?

The usual practice is for the most senior member of staff (the Director, Chief Executive, Co-ordinator or whatever she or he is titled) to participate in meetings. Other staff members may be involved as follows:

- To attend regularly because of their particular role (e.g. a Finance Director may need to attend to provide information to the Treasurer and the committee).
- To attend, by invitation, when matters of direct concern or that person's area of work are under discussion.

Some organisations involve the whole of their senior management team in managing committee meetings.

Making your meetings lively and effective

The managing committee operates through meetings. It is most effective when its members are able to work together in an atmosphere of trust and commitment to achieve agreed results. To succeed it needs to have:

1. Appropriate members – with the skills and experience needed.

2. Clear purpose.

3. Simple, clear structure and size – a reasonable upper limit for size is around 12-15 members, bigger committees face more problems.

4. An effective chair.

5. Appropriate processes for discussion and decision making.

6. A positive atmosphere.

7. Good record keeping (minutes) and administration (agendas and relevant papers).

8. An expectation that decisions will be implemented (i.e. an orientation towards results).

Points 1 to 4 are covered elsewhere in "*The Effective Trustee*" series. Here we concentrate on the processes you might use to make your meetings sparkle and to keep good records. For more details on this see *Books 2, 3 and 5* in *Chapter 10*. You may find it helpful to assess your meetings using process described on page 15.

Committee processes

Managing committees are affected by a strange phenomenon – the "brain in the bag syndrome" in which an otherwise lively group of people, each committed to the cause, each with ample skills and experience, becomes stultified and half paralysed the moment it gets into a committee meeting. Each person appears to leave their brain in the bag from which they take their papers. Sharp, incisive minds become leaden and woolly; people with vast financial experience agree to sums which don't add up; effective communicators babble incoherently, and above all, everyone behaves as though it doesn't really matter because it's all somebody else's responsibility.

The managing committee must be regarded as a team of people with a complex and responsible job to do. Many committees fail to clear their first two hurdles: they fail to appoint suitably skilled people (or train people to have suitable skills), and they fail to explain what it is the committee has to do. Assuming the committee is properly set up, what steps should you take to ensure a lively and effective meeting? Here are some ideas:

1. Give a **clear job description** to members, so they know what they are supposed to do.

2. Provide **induction**, so each knows enough about the organisation and the committee to do their job.

3. Make sure members know enough **about each other** to make use of their various skills.

4. Check or audit the **skills and experience** on the committee.

5. Explain the **purpose of each meeting** and each item on the agenda. Involve those members with relevant skills/experience in discussing each item.

6. Provide appropriate **papers and information** to support each item on the agenda.

7. Create a climate in which each member of the committee is expected to have **read the papers** and prepared for the meeting.

(continues on page 18)

Finding the right process for meetings

1. Agree the ground rules.

Ensure that everyone knows and agrees the **ground rules** for the meetings, such as:

- It's OK to ask questions.
- If in doubt, ask.
- Keep contributions brief and to the point.
- Do not repeat other people's contributions.
- Listen to people's contributions.
- Don't interrupt.
- Don't use jargon and abbreviations unless they are explained.
- Be open and honest with each other.

This process need not take long but may serve as a helpful reminder and set a tone for the meeting.

2. Improve relationships

Give people a chance to get to know each other outside the formal business of committee meetings.

3. Explain why the committee is working in a particular way

The Chair should explain why the committee works the way it does. If it is a large committee, things may have to be quite formal. As long as people know this they can adapt and cope. If a less formal style is being used for a particular item, make sure people know why.

4. Review how things have gone in meetings each year

Allow time to review the way the committee meetings have worked each year. Use the review to plan ways to improve.

ACTIVITY

How good are your meetings?

Read through the points listed below, and tick the appropriate box for each:

	Usually	Sometimes	Rarely
Purpose			
The reason for the meeting is clear.	☐	☐	☐
The reason for each item on the agenda is clear.	☐	☐	☐
The results expected from the meeting are clear.	☐	☐	☐
Environment			
The room used for the meeting is comfortable and has enough air, light and heat.	☐	☐	☐
The furniture is arranged in a way which gets the best out of people.	☐	☐	☐
People			
The people present have the skills and knowledge to get through the agenda effectively.	☐	☐	☐
The people work well together, making use of each other's skills.	☐	☐	☐
People behave well at meetings, keeping contributions brief and to the point.	☐	☐	☐
All members take part in discussions.	☐	☐	☐
The membership of the committee shows an appropriate balance of gender, race, age and experience.	☐	☐	☐
Time			
There is enough time for the meetings.	☐	☐	☐
Meetings do not drag on too long.	☐	☐	☐
Time within meetings is well used.	☐	☐	☐
The meetings are held at an appropriate time of day, and on a suitable day of the week.	☐	☐	☐
Information			
Information for the meeting is circulated well in advance.	☐	☐	☐
Every paper has a clear purpose, and spells out the main points for the managing committee to consider.	☐	☐	☐
Papers are not presented at the meeting except in absolute emergencies.	☐	☐	☐
Papers are clear and intelligible, and not riddled with jargon.	☐	☐	☐
Committee members read papers in advance of meetings.	☐	☐	☐

How good are your meetings? *(continued)*

ACTIVITY

	Usually	Sometimes	Rarely
The Agenda			
Matters arising from the previous meeting are discussed and followed up.	☐	☐	☐
The agenda is well ordered, with important matters first.	☐	☐	☐
The agenda is realistic and is usually completed on time.	☐	☐	☐
Atmosphere			
Meetings have a relaxed but purposeful atmosphere.	☐	☐	☐
People are listened to.	☐	☐	☐
Members are friendly and welcoming.	☐	☐	☐
All members feel positively about the meetings and their own role.	☐	☐	☐
Process			
Adequate time is given for discussion.	☐	☐	☐
Matters are explained or elaborated on, where necessary.	☐	☐	☐
Agenda items move from discussion to clear decisions.	☐	☐	☐
Tasks for follow up are allocated.	☐	☐	☐
A variety of processes is used to ensure effective discussions.	☐	☐	☐
Special meetings are held to discuss particular things such as strategy, budgets, etc.	☐	☐	☐
Records			
Decisions are summarised at the meeting.	☐	☐	☐
Minutes are circulated soon after the meeting.	☐	☐	☐
The minutes identify who will take what action, and when.	☐	☐	☐
Costs			
The cost of the meetings is assessed and kept under review.	☐	☐	☐
Sufficient investment is made in the meetings to ensure they are effective (e.g. room hire, catering, travel expenses).	☐	☐	☐
The amount of time trustees can devote to meetings is understood.	☐	☐	☐
Trustees are not overloaded.	☐	☐	☐

8. Emphasise that the committee members **are responsible** for the organisation's affairs.

9. Make sure members do not **over-commit themselves** or become overloaded with work.

10. Pay attention to the **rewards** that members get from doing their work well. Make sure it does not become a tedious chore.

Decision making

Most governing instruments require decisions to be made by simple majority voting. This means putting decisions to the vote. If a majority is in favour, the decision is carried.

In practice, most managing committees make decisions by general agreement and

ACTIVITY

Meeting Blockers

Read the list of things that prevent effective meetings given below. Tick any that seem to apply to your committee. Identify how you could reduce or overcome such blocks in future.

☐ **Fear**
Fear that the decision will bring horrible consequences, such as conflict, criticism or disagreement.

☐ **Lack of commitment**
Members do not really care about the decision. It's not really their organisation after all. The committee does not feel responsible. It usually leaves it all to the officers or the staff.

☐ **Exposed as "managers"**
Some committees live in terror of being seen as "managers" or in charge of the organisation. They would lose all their street credibility.

☐ **Conflict of interest**
Members are unable to separate other, conflicting interests from their role as trustees of the organisation. They argue for the interests of their own organisation or group.

☐ **Interpersonal conflict**
When people start to fight it creates a tense, unsafe atmosphere in which the free exchange of ideas and opinions becomes very difficult.

☐ **Hidden agenda**
Members think other members are hatching a plot, for reasons that are not out in the open. Often occurs when there are power struggles, or conflicting ideologies on the committee.

☐ **Lousy chairing**
A poor chair can prevent good decisions from being reached by stopping discussion too soon; allowing it to wander; rushing to a decision; bullying; not summarising; forgetting to move to a decision.

☐ **Rigid methods**
Some decisions need time, space and an atmosphere that is different to the typical committee meeting.

☐ **Erratic attendance**
Committees struggle when they never have the same people at successive meetings. There is no cohesion, and old decisions are frequently discussed again and may be reversed.

☐ **Lack of cohesion**
If the committee is not able to function as a team, its decision making powers will be impaired.

☐ **Lack of information**
It is not possible to make good decisions without adequate information.

☐ **Poor description of the matter to be decided**
The first ingredient of a good decision is a clear and accurate description of the problem or issue that you need to decide. Many managing committees end up making decisions about the wrong problems.

Others
Add any others that affect your committee:

rarely go to a vote. This is fine when there is a consensus, but can lead to problems when this is not the case. the Chair should make sure that:

- The decision to which members are being asked to agree is clear.
- Views for and against the decision have been heard.
- There is real agreement on the decision.

- If views are split, the meeting can move to a vote, if necessary.
- Voting is minuted if anyone requests this, so that any dissenting members can record their disagreement.

Types of decision-making

TECHNICAL DETAIL

True consensus *(everyone in favour)*

Full agreement of all committee members, after full discussion of all the various views and ideas. Involves compromise and listening, and takes time. In true consensus, everyone fully supports the decision that has to be made. It is not enough just to not disagree.

Silent consensus *(no-one against)*

It seems that everyone is in favour, but this has not been properly checked. Some members may have kept quiet, not felt able to disagree, needed more time to think, etc.

Silent consensus may be reached by the Chair saying "is there anyone against?".

Majority decision

In larger committees, this may be the only way to get decisions. Usually a vote is used. Majority decisions can create disaffected minorities. In a democratic system, the minority is bound to follow the decision of the majority, until such time as the decision can be altered. In a managing committee, all share responsibility for the decisions made.

Minority decision

A minority makes the decision and the majority lets them. Minority decision making creates divisions in the committee and can lead to the majority losing interest.

Individual dominance

The decision is made by one person. The committee allows it to happen. This can occur when the Chair thinks that everyone is involved, but the other members are just doing what they think she wants.

No decision

The decision is made by not making a decision – nothing is done. New ideas or questions fall into a bottomless pit. This is often seen in organisations which have lost direction – no decision is made to alter the direction, or even to discuss the problem. Questions like *"why are we doing this?"* or *"how will this help us to achieve our aims?"*, fall into the pit and vanish for ever.

A simple guide for making decisions by consensus

1. What are we trying to decide?
   Be sure this is clear to everyone.
2. What are the different possibilities?
   Consider as many as possible.
3. How may each possibility work?
   Discuss the pros and cons.
4. What suggestions, or combination of suggestions, do we choose?
5. What do we need to carry out the decision?
6. Who will do what? When? Where and How?

Based on ideas in *"Training for Transformation"*, Hope et al, Mambo Press 1984

Checklist for taking decisions

- Why is a decision needed? What is the real problem you are trying to solve?
- What would happen if you did nothing?
- What is the worst thing that could happen if you made a bad decision?
- Do you need more information? If so, in what form?
- Have you met this problem before?
  How did you solve it then?
- Does the committee use a variety of methods to enable it to produce really creative solutions to problems?
- Does the committee consider a variety of possible solutions?
- Have all the different views been heard?
- How do you choose the best solution?
- Do you usually reach clear, appropriate decisions which can be acted upon?
- What are the costs of the decision (time, money, etc.)?
- Who will be responsible for seeing that the decision implemented?
- How will you communicate the decisions to others – staff, members, users, etc.?

Effective meetings

- Do committee members understand their role and responsibilities?
- Does the committee contain all the skills, experience and expertise it needs to do its job?
- Is the size of the committee appropriate and effective?
- Is the purpose of the meeting clear?
- Is there a properly prepared agenda?
- Are supporting papers provided?
- Does each item have a clear purpose?
- Is time well allocated to important items?
- Is the Chair competent to run the meeting?
- Is every member able to contribute?
- Is the atmosphere constructive and open?
- Do members work well together as a team?
- Is discussion summarised before moving to a decision?
- Do decisions receive the genuine support of the whole committee?
- Is the process used for the meetings reviewed regularly?
- Are processes used which generate energy and enthusiasm?

Jargon and bad language

TECHNICAL DETAIL

Many people new to committees will not be familiar with the weird and wonderful language that is commonly used. The golden rule is – if in doubt, ask. You cannot carry out your role as a trustee if you do not really understand what is going on. Encourage people not to use jargon and to explain any acronyms or abbreviations that they use. The table below explains some of the common committee terms.

Term	*Explanation*
Amendment	A suggested change to a proposal or motion. In a formal meeting, the amendment will be prepared and seconded.
Casting vote	The Chair of the meeting has a second vote, in the case of a tied vote.
Chair's powers	The power given to the Chair, by the managing committee, to make decisions on urgent matters between meetings. The Chair must report back on such decisions.
Ex officio	This means "by virtue of the office held". Many committees have ex officio members such as the Chair of another organisation, or the Director of a Social Services department. Do not confuse ex officio with non-voting or "unofficial" members.
Motion	A proposal which is presented for discussion and requires a decision. In formal meetings a motion may need to have a formal proposer and seconder.
Officers	The Chair, Vice-Chairs, Secretary and Treasurer of the organisation. The officers may be given powers in the governing instrument to act on behalf of the managing committee.
Proposal	A specific course of action put forward by an individual at the meeting.
Proposer	A person who proposes a specific course of action. The proposer is usually asked to explain their proposal.
Quorum	The minimum number of members of the managing committee who must attend before the meeting is valid. The quorum is set out in the constitution.
Through the Chair	Archaic way of politely directing a comment to the whole meeting, through the authority of the Chair.
Seconder	A person who formally supports the proposer of the motion. The seconder usually speaks in favour of the proposed action.
Standing orders	A set of rules for conducting committee meetings or general meetings. They are usually written as an appendix to the governing instrument. Or they may be contained within the governing instrument.

Self-assessment

Organising your meetings

		Know	Must check
1.	Do you know the rules for your managing committee meetings laid down in your governing instrument.	☐	☐
2.	Can you identify ten good reasons for holding managing committee meetings!	☐	☐
3.	What steps can a managing committee take to enable it to work better as a team.	☐	☐
4.	What are the essential ingredients of an effective agenda.	☐	☐
5.	What is an annual cycle of meetings? Why should managing committees have one?	☐	☐
6.	What is an effective size for a managing committee?	☐	☐
7.	What are the advantages of setting up sub-committees?	☐	☐
8.	What is the difference between a sub-committee and a working group?	☐	☐
9.	In what ways can staff be involved on the managing committee?	☐	☐
10.	What eight steps can you take to ensure your meetings are lively and effective?	☐	☐

Working with paid staff

NEED TO KNOW

Your responsibilities

When a voluntary organisation decides to employ paid staff, the managing committee takes on the role of employer. The relationship between the managing committee, who are all volunteers, and the professional, paid staff is critical to the success of the organisation.

Your **TRUSTEE** responsibilities are to make sure that the organisation *obeys the law* regarding employment of staff, and especially that:

- Staff have proper *contracts of employment.*
- *Equal opportunities* legislation is understood and acted upon.
- Staff are paid and *PAYE and National Insurance* deductions are paid to the Inland Revenue.
- The organisation and its staff are properly *insured.*
- *Health and safety* rules are obeyed.
- Specific *requirements* affecting the work of the organisation are obeyed (such as the Children Act when working with children, or Food Hygiene Regulations when providing cooked meals).

Your **MANAGEMENT** responsibilities are to see that the organisation is a *good employer* and especially that:

- The organisation has appropriate *policies and procedures* for managing its staff.
- Staff are *paid* at an appropriate level.
- Sufficient resources are provided to *train and develop* staff.
- Staff work to an appropriate *standard and quality.*
- Staff are properly *supervised* and *account* regularly for their work.
- The organisation uses a style of management in keeping with its values and aims.
- The managing committee establishes a clear and effective relationship with the *senior staff member* (the Director or Chief Executive) or with the staff team.

The legal requirements for employers

The managing committee becomes an employer as soon as paid staff are hired. You need to be aware of the legal requirements for employing people which you must obey. Your role as employer should be taken very seriously for three reasons:

- You are responsible for seeing that staff work effectively towards achieving the objects of the organisation. If they don't, you are not managing the organisation's resources effectively;
- Staff rely on you for their livelihood.
- Your organisation may face serious penalties if you do not obey the laws covering employment. In some circumstances you might face personal

liability for debts that result from mismanagement of staff or failure to adhere to employment legislation *(see Book 6)*.

The trustee role as employer is affected by a large number of pieces of legislation. Trustees do not need to know the detail of every act, but must be sure that the organisation is aware of their main requirements. Make sure the organisation is up to date with changes in the law. Some managing committees delegate the task of keeping fully informed on legal matters to their legal

TECHNICAL DETAIL

The main legislation affecting employers in England and Wales

1 The Employment Protection (Consolidation) Act 1978:

Every employee working more than 16 hours per week is entitled to a **written contract** of employment.

2 The Health and Safety at Work Act 1974:

Lays down requirements to ensure a **safe and healthy workplace**.

This includes a written Health and Safety policy (if there are more than 5 employees); a named person responsible for Health and Safety; procedures for recording accidents; a description of arrangements for consultation with trade unions; procedures for informing staff of health and safety matters.

3 The Office, Shops and Railway Premises Act 1963

Require a clean, safe **working environment**. It specifies that premises must be heated to at least 16 degrees Celsius after the first hour of work.

4 Sex Discrimination Act 1975 and the Race Relations Act 1976.

These make it an **offence to discriminate** directly or indirectly on the grounds of race, colour, ethnic origin, nationality, national origin, sex or marital status, except where these are genuine occupational qualifications for a job.

The Race Relations Act does not cover Northern Ireland. A separate order extends the Sex Discrimination Act to Northern Ireland. In addition, organisations are required to obey the **Fair Employment (NI) Act 1989** which prohibits direct or indirect discrimination on the grounds of religion. All employers with 10 employees must monitor the religious make up of the workforce each year.

5 The Equal Pay Act 1970

Requires that men and women receive **equal pay** for equivalent work or work of the same nature.

6 The Disabled Persons (Employment) Act 1944

Where employers have more than 20 staff, at least 3% of the workforce must be made up of registered **disabled people,** unless an exemption is granted.

7 Rehabilitation of Offenders Act 1974

Entitles people not to reveal certain criminal convictions which are considered "spent" after a certain length of time. Longer prison sentences for serious crimes are never spent. Short sentences may be spent after 5 or 10 years. Employment in the social services field is usually exempt from the Act. This means candidates for employment **can** be asked to disclose all previous criminal convictions.

8 Social Security Act 1975

Requires the employer to inform employees whether they are contracted out of the **state pension scheme**.

9 The Employment Acts 1980, 1982 and 1993 and Trade Union Act 1984

These limit employees rights to picket or conduct **secondary industrial action**, regulate trade union ballots and effectively outlaw the closed shop.

For more detail on employment legislation see *Book 6* in *Chapter 10*.

advisor, or to a suitably qualified member of the committee or staff.

The duty of care

In addition to specific legislation, the managing committee has a duty to make sure that staff, volunteers and clients are not put at unreasonable risk. This is known as the duty of care. The managing committee must be able to show that the activities and behaviour of the staff and volunteers are organised in ways that would be considered to be reasonable. Each trustee must behave in a way that would be considered reasonable for someone fulfilling the role of a trustee. The duty of care needs to be taken very seriously, particularly where the organisation works with vulnerable people. See *Book 6* in *Chapter 10*.

Employment rights

Committee members should be aware of the rights their employees are afforded in law. These are statutory minimums and must be ensured. Most charitable organisations will wish to become "good employers", to treat their staff with respect and dignity, and to offer good terms and conditions of employment. Developing enlightened employment policies is a means of ensuring that the organisation provides high quality services to its beneficiaries, by maintaining a well-trained motivated workforce.

You and the other trustees must always keep in mind that the resources of the charity must only be used to the benefit of the beneficiaries. Avoid being drawn towards employment practices that, however laudable, appear to be solely in the interests of the staff.

The Charity Commission is entitled to question "ex gratia" payments made by charities to staff members, over and above that which is required by law. Such payments are not generally allowed. If you have any doubts about your employment practice, always check with your legal advisors or with the Charity Commission.

Legal aspects of employment

CHECK POINT

- Who is responsible for ensuring that the organisation is fully informed about its legal obligations as an employer? How is the information communicated to the managing committee?

- Who is responsible for seeing that the organisation is meeting all its legal requirements as an employer?

- Are you confident that the managing committee is carrying out its duty of care towards staff, volunteers and users of the organisation?

- Is the detailed work of being an employer delegated by the managing committee? If so, to whom is it delegated? Does the managing committee receive adequate reports about employment matters?

- Does the organisation have appropriate policies and procedures for handling staffing matters? Are these policies and procedures reviewed periodically?

Trade union rights

Your staff are entitled to belong or to choose not to belong, to a trade union. Staff who are union members are entitled to take part in trade union activities. These can be held during work time, if this is agreed by the managing committee.

If several staff join the same union, they may wish to have it officially recognised by the managing committee. Managing committees are not obliged to recognise any trade unions. If recognition is granted, the union is entitled to negotiate over terms and conditions of employment.

If there is more than one union, the managing committee may decide to recognise the one with the largest membership. An alternative is for the unions to form a joint negotiating committee.

ACTIVITY

Practical aspects of employment

The managing committee is responsible for fulfilling the legal duties and responsibilities of an employer. Larger organisations will have a personnel manager. In smaller organisations, this responsibility is usually delegated to particular committee members, such as the Treasurer or the Secretary. *See Books 9,10,11 and 12* in *Chapter 10* for more details.

Read the checklist below and tick the boxes as appropriate:

Does your organisation:	Yes	Not sure	Have someone responsible
Provide contracts of employment including terms and conditions of service	☐	☐	☐
Provide itemised pay statements	☐	☐	☐
Provide statutory sick pay	☐	☐	☐
Send PAYE and National Insurance contributions to Inland Revenue on time	☐	☐	☐
Provide pensions (or not, as the case may be)	☐	☐	☐
Keep a record of temporary and casual staff	☐	☐	☐
Maintain a safe and healthy workplace	☐	☐	☐
Provide proper insurance cover	☐	☐	☐
Keep an accident book	☐	☐	☐
Allow trade union involvement	☐	☐	☐
Have formal procedures for grievances or disciplinary action	☐	☐	☐
Monitor job applicants and post holders for equal opportunities	☐	☐	☐

For more detail on the legal aspects of employment see *Book 1* in *Chapter 10*.

Establishing a staffing policy

The staff of an organisation are its single biggest resource. They represent an asset which should be managed and developed for the benefit of the organisation. Staff are not just a cost. The managing committee should establish a framework of policies to guide the management of its staff. Three of the most important policies are:

- **A staff development policy**. This covers all aspects of the organisation's approach to staffing matters.

- **An equal opportunities policy.** Aims to make sure that staff are appointed fairly and do not suffer unfair discrimination in their work. Whilst it may focus on staffing matters, the equal opportunities policy should extend to all aspects of the organisation's work, such as ensuring that services are provided on fair grounds, or that staff do not behave in discriminatory ways.

- **A pay policy.** Deciding the rates of pay for staff and the procedure for regulating these. This should be agreed through a suitable process of consultation with staff representatives or relevant trade unions. Some organisations link the pay of their staff to that of staff in local authority employment. Others choose to set rates of pay they judge to be appropriate for the type of work involved, and for their area.

These policies provide a framework to respond to issues and problems as they arise, rather than relying on solutions made up as you go along.

Staff development

Effective organisations recognise the need to invest in their people. They nurture them by providing opportunities for learning and development which encourage:

- Personal and professional development.
- Improved performance.
- People to work better together as a team.
- The organisation to adapt and develop in response to changing needs, demands and circumstances.

Staff development is often tackled under the following headings:

- **Recruitment and selection**: fairly attracting and choosing staff with the right skills and qualities for the work.
- **Induction:** preparing staff properly for their work.

- **Supervision**: ensuring that staff are adequately supervised and can learn from the work that they do.
- **Training and development:** encouraging all staff to train and pursue their career and professional development.

A **staff development policy** commits the organisation to investing resources in its staff. Such a policy might provide:

- A **training budget** for staff and volunteers. Some organisations allocate an amount such as 3% of their annual turnover for training, with the training to take place in paid work time.
- Time set aside for **supervision** with effective systems and procedures for managing staff.

Equal opportunities

All charities have a responsibility to see that their services are provided fairly to those who need them. One important step is to establish an **equal opportunities policy.** Part of such a policy will lead you to ensure that staff are employed fairly. Your equal opportunities in employment policy should make sure that no member of staff suffers direct or indirect discrimination on unfair grounds. This can be implemented by:

- Advertising **job vacancies** openly and widely.
- Adopting **selection procedures** which are fair and focus on the job to be done.
- Using **procedures for supervision** and training which are fair and focus on the development of skills to carry out the work.
- Adopting **flexible working practices** – job-sharing, flexi-time, etc.
- Taking account of **child care** needs.
- Making sure that premises are **physically accessible** to disabled people.

27

- Making sure that the **working environment** has been adapted to meet the needs of people with sensory disabilities, such deafness.
- **Monitoring** how the policy affects the make up of the staff; who gets promotion; who gets training; etc.

The equal opportunities policy should be monitored. This involves keeping records, broken down by gender, age, ethnic origin, race, religion (in N. Ireland) disability and other appropriate grounds. Monitoring could cover:

- Job applicants.
- People shortlisted for jobs.
- People appointed.
- Staff as a whole.
- Volunteers.
- Managing committee members.
- Service users.

Pay policy

Pay is often the biggest single item of expenditure for a voluntary organisation. The trustees need to know the **basis on which decisions about pay are made** or have been made in the past. A pay policy might include:

- **Linking pay** to that of other, similar organisations (such as local authority pay scales).
- **Rewarding performance** (payment by results), competence (more pay for staff who achieve higher levels of competence).
- Ensuring that pay is not isolated from other, more **personal rewards**, such as professional training and development, job development, responsibility, etc.

For any particular job, the trustees should consider:

- What other jobs are similar to the job in question and the rate of pay for similar jobs in other organisations.
- What other people in the organisation get paid and how the job in question relates to these other jobs – internal differentials.
- What the organisation can actually afford to pay.
- What the organisation must pay to attract applicants of the right calibre.
- What agreements already exist with staff and trade unions on rates of pay.

Some voluntary organisations pay quite low wages in comparison to the public and private sectors. This is changing, as more staff move from one sector to another. Paying low wages can be a very short-term, false economy. Low wages may lead to high staff turnover, loss of key staff, high costs in recruiting new staff, low morale among staff, loss of continuity in work and so on.

Trustees have a duty to ensure that the charity's money is used to best effect. You should be sure that paying staff at whatever level you decide will lead to the most effective use of the charity's resources. Levels of pay should neither be too high, nor too low.

PAYE

The managing committee is responsible for paying the Inland Revenue the Income Tax and National Insurance that is due, and to ensure that this is done on time. The organisation faces severe penalties if it fails to do this. See *Book 9* in *Chapter 10*.

Being a good employer

Any organisation employing staff will need to have adequate procedures to:

- **Analyse** what work needs to be done by staff.
- Produce accurate and realistic **job descriptions** and **person specifications** for these jobs when making appointments.

- **Recruit** suitably qualified staff.
- Ensure that new staff have a **proper induction** to their work and to the organisation.
- **Pay and reward** staff appropriately.
- **Manage the performance of staff,** including setting realistic objectives and monitoring progress towards their achievement.
- **Train and develop** staff.
- **Communicate effectively** with staff.

There is a double role: firstly to ensure that there are proper procedures for supervising and managing the staff; and secondly to supervise and manage the staff. All trustees are responsible for seeing that there are proper procedures in place. Whether they do the actual day-to-day management of staff or not will depend on the size of the organisation.

Large organisations will be employing hundreds or even thousands of staff, and personnel management will be delegated to the Director and then to the Head of Personnel. For smaller organisations, senior staff (either the Director or the Administrator) will still be doing most of the actual management work. For quite small organisations, the committee itself may try to do most of the work. This imposes a considerable burden, and it is usually more satisfactory to delegate as much as possible to the senior staff member.

The staffing sub-committee

Staffing matters can absorb a large amount of the committee's time. One solution is to delegate responsibility for this to a staffing sub-committee. This can be smaller, and can include people with

Staffing policies

CHECK POINT

- How does your managing committee keep itself informed about the law affecting employment?

- How does your organisation deal with staffing matters?
  Is each issue dealt with as it arises, on an ad hoc basis?

- Does your organisation have a policy for staffing? Does the policy cover: rates of pay; terms and conditions of service; procedures for recruitment; induction; supervision; training and development?

- Is there an equal opportunities policy?
  What plans are there for its implementation?
  How is the policy monitored?

- What resources are set aside to ensure your staff can train and develop?

- Does your organisation have a policy on pay?
  How are levels of pay decided and agreed?

- Are staff paid at a level which ensures that the organisation is able to work most effectively?

particular skills and experience of staffing issues. The senior staff member will usually be a member of this sub-committee, but may be asked to leave meetings when matters concerning her or his employment are being discussed.

The staffing sub-committee should be given a very clear brief and report back regularly to the managing committee, which still has the ultimate responsibility for the staff.

As a trustee, your essential task is to **see that staff are properly managed,** rather than trying to manage them yourself. The key to doing this well is to make sure that you are clear what needs to be done; that you delegate the tasks well; and that you receive regular, appropriate information on progress.

29

Accountability

The trustees are ultimately accountable for the organisation. If the buck has to stop, it stops with them. In practice, much of the day-to-day work of an organisation (which employs staff) will be delegated to the staff. There are two critical factors:

- **Clear lines of accountability.**
  Make sure you are absolutely clear who is accountable to whom. This means having a clear map of accountability, for example, a diagram of the structure of the organisation. Every time you notice a person who appears to be accountable to more than one person, you should check to see that relationships are clear. The greater the level of confusion, the more room there is for people to just "do their own thing". As trustees, you must be certain that people are working towards the objects of your charity and in the best interests of your beneficiaries.
- **A good working relationship** with the senior staff member. The senior staff member is the link point between the staff team and the committee. On almost all matters, the staff will be accountable directly or indirectly to the senior staff member, who in turn will be accountable to the committee. The committee must be able to supervise and manage the senior staff member effectively. It must also develop a good working relationship with the senior staff member, with mutual agreement on the division of roles and responsibilities.

Recruitment and induction

Recruitment and induction of staff are discussed in *Chapter 5*.

Supervision of the senior staff member

The supervision of the senior staff member is fraught with difficulty. The process lies at the heart of the relationship between the managing committee and the staff as a whole. The relationship has many possible tensions and problems because it involves both **judgement** of performance and **counselling** with regard to work related problems, and personal needs. Other tensions include:

- The senior staff member is a professional. None of the managing committee may have the relevant professional expertise.
- The managing committee will often know less than the senior staff member about the affairs of the organisation.
- The managing committee is the employer.
- The managing committee may include members with whom the senior staff member works on a professional basis. It may not be appropriate to discuss personal issues or professional problems in front of them.
- The committee may have members from organisations which are in competition.

The tensions can be minimised by separating the different aspects of supervision. These include reviewing the work done; assessing progress towards agreed objectives; and identifying personal training and development needs for the senior staff member to become even more effective in the job.

Supervision of the staff

In all but the smallest organisations, responsibility for the supervision of the staff will be delegated to the senior staff member. She or he directly supervises some staff, and they may in turn supervise others.

The managing committee should be confident that the organisation has adequate systems for the supervision of the staff. These should deal effectively with both **control and monitoring of staff performance**, and with enabling staff to **learn, grow and develop.**

Division of roles between staff and managing committee

The **committee**:

- Is responsible for the organisation.
- Safeguards the values and purpose of the organisation.
- Checks activities contribute to achieving the objects.
- Decides the policies which provide a framework for the work of staff and volunteers.
- Decides overall aims and objectives, priorities and strategy.
- Employs the staff.
- Monitors progress towards the objectives, requires reports and information.
- Evaluates progress.
- Provides recognition and feedback to staff and volunteers.
- Delegates day-to-day work to staff, volunteers, sub-committees and working groups.

The **senior staff member** with assistance from staff and volunteers:

- Carries out the work of the organisation.
- Reports regularly on achievements and progress.
- Makes decisions, where the power to do this has been delegated.
- Provides information on issues, problems and policy matters, and makes recommendations for the committee to consider.
- Draws up plans for the future development of the organisation's work for the committee to decide upon.

- Advises and informs the committee, so that it is able to carry out its governing role.

The **committee** focus lies in keeping an overview, ensuring clear direction and overall plans, and making sure resources are properly and well used.

The **staff and volunteers** (including those committee members who contribute beyond their supervisory role) do the day-to-day work. They make decisions where they are delegated the power to do so, provide reports, and importantly provide reasoned information, advice and recommendations on matters which the committee must decide.

To make the relationship between staff and the committee effective, the **committee members** must have:

- A shared vision for the organisation, which is then shared with the staff.
- A commitment to achieving the objectives of the organisation.
- Well understood trustee roles, so that they do not interfere inappropriately in the day-to-day running of the organisation.
- Confidence in the abilities of the staff, and willingness to back the judgement of their staff in the event of problems, provided they have been kept informed.
- Good information for decisions which have to be made.

There is no single right way to manage staff. You should use an approach which fits the values and style of your organisation. If the system emphasises control and monitoring, you may create a climate in which staff are told what to do, are expected to perform to set standards, and are not expected to use much initiative or imagination. If the system emphasises development, staff may be encouraged to set their own standards, take risks, learn from mistakes, participate in the organisation's decision making and so on. Staff may need training to ensure that they have the skills to be effective supervisors. The managing committee will want to make sure that there is an adequate training budget for this and that it is used effectively.

TECHNICAL DETAIL

Ways of supervising your senior staff member

There are several ways to supervise your organisation's senior staff member. Supervision can be done by:

1 The committee as a whole

This is not usually effective, but can sometimes work in small, informal organisations. It may be quite inappropriate if the committee contains people to whom it would be unwise, or unprofessional for the senior staff member to confide problems.

The committee is ultimately accountable for the performance of the senior staff member and should always carry out an overall monitoring role.

2 The Chair

This is the most common arrangement. The Chair must have the necessary skills, knowledge and time to do it.

3 An employment or staff sub-committee

This can sometimes work, but supervision by a group brings its own problems as with supervision by the whole managing committee.

4 A suitably skilled committee member

The keys here are the terms of the supervision arrangement and the level of confidentiality. How much will be reported back to the committee as a whole? What authority does the supervisor have?

5 An external consultant with appropriate skills

This costs money. Your organisation would need to establish very clearly the terms of the supervision. What, if anything, would be reported back to the managing committee?

6 A peer, in another organisation

This again raises questions of confidentiality. A peer in a similar organisation may be the only person who has a real professional understanding of the work the Chief Executive is doing.

Some organisations use a combination of different methods.

Management style

There is no single, right way to manage staff. The managing committee is responsible for making sure that the organisation is managed effectively. This means that it achieves its objectives, in the short and long term.

Appraisal of staff performance

Trustees should see that there is a system for **appraisal** of staff performance. This is usually done each year, and involves assessing how effective each member of staff has been in their work. This sort of appraisal works best when:

- There is an atmosphere of trust and honesty.
- The person being supervised is involved in assessing their own performance.
- The appraisal is linked to training and development, rather than to pay and reward.

The managing committee is directly responsible for the performance of the senior staff member. Most managing committees delegate this task to the Chair, or to a small sub-committee.

For more on appraisal see *Book 13* in *Chapter 10*.

Ways of giving supervision

Supervision can take place in a variety of ways. It need not rely only on formal, planned meetings.

1. Informal but planned

Staff and their manager agree objectives for both their work and their own development. Managers give supervision to staff about the agreed objectives during everyday contact with one another.

2. Informal and unplanned.

Managers take whatever opportunity arises to supervise their staff.

3. Formal and regular

Regular meetings between individual staff and their manager.

4. Formal but irregular

Meetings set up from time to time to discuss matters that have become pressing. This is typically in response to problems.

The important thing is to make sure that each member of staff is clear what it is they are supposed to be doing and has sufficient, high quality contact with their manager to enable them to do it well.

TECHNICAL DETAIL

Training

Staff should be properly trained and able to do the work that is required of them. Training provides an important tool for achieving good quality work.

You should see that the organisation sets aside appropriate resources to enable the training of its staff and volunteers. The training of trustees should be included within this budget.

It is helpful to develop a training strategy for the organisation, so that the use of limited resources can be planned to best effect.

Managing poor performance

It is better to encourage good, effective work by staff and volunteers than to be thrown in to a crisis by poor performance. The managing committee should see that the organisation has an adequate system for managing the work of staff and volunteers.

Your organisation should have a procedure for dealing with poor performance even if you manage to avoid ever having to use it. The last thing your organisations needs when faced with poor performance is to find that there is no procedure to deal with it. It is best to use a stage-by-stage approach. Make sure your staff and volunteers are aware of the process your organisation uses.

Working with your staff

CHECK POINT

- Does your organisation produce job descriptions and job specifications for all posts? Who is responsible for doing this?
- Are new staff given induction into their posts and the organisation?
- Are staff supervised regularly?
- Is the senior staff member supervised regularly? By whom?
- Does your organisation carry out regular appraisal of the staff? Who is responsible for this?
- Is money allocated in the budget for training and developing the staff?
- Is there a clear division of roles between the managing committee and the staff?

TECHNICAL DETAIL

Examples of management styles

In order to achieve the organisation's objectives staff must be motivated. Styles of management vary between focusing mainly on the job to be done (sometimes at the expense of the people who do it), through to focusing mainly on the needs of the staff (sometimes at the expense of getting the job done). Different styles are needed for different situations.

Organisations often need different styles at different stages in their development.

1. Directing

Suitable for staff who are fairly inexperienced, and need a clear description of what to do, how, when, etc.

This style can lead to an authoritarian approach. People are told what to do rather than being involved in decisions. This can be suitable when dealing with crises and emergencies, but may be more limited in other situations.

2. Coaching

Suitable when a staff member has reasonable experience, and some skills. She needs space to get on with the job, but also regular advice and guidance on how to do it.

In an organisation this style may lead to a teamwork approach. People work in teams and learn from each other through working together. Team leaders are expected to give advice and guidance.

3. Supporting

The staff member is given space to carry out the job. She may decide much of the content of the job herself. The manager works with her to enable her to solve problems.

Organisations with this style tend to be very developmental. They are concerned with the growth and development of the staff, as this will lead to more effective work.

4. Delegating

Staff are given a job to do and delegated the power to get on and do it. Minimal support and guidance is given. This works well when staff are both competent and confident to cope with the responsibility they have been given.

This style is found in entrepreneurial organisations in which staff are given a great deal of room to make their own running. As little support is given, if it is used inappropriately, this style of management can lead to stress and burn out.

For more on management style see *Book 7* in *Chapter 10.*

What is poor performance?

The managing committee may be concerned about the performance of a staff member or volunteer if:

- Work is not done to the required standard.
- Work does not meet agreed targets or objectives.
- The staff member seems to have problems working effectively with others in the organisation.
- The staff member does not seem to be carrying out their contracted hours.
- There is adverse feedback, from more than one source, about the staff member's work.

There may be many causes of a dip in performance. The first response is to explore possible reasons with the person concerned and see if things can be put right.

Encouraging the best from your staff and volunteers:

1. Set realistic objectives

Each person should have clear, realistic objectives for her or his work. These should be focused on achieving specified results, with an emphasis on the quality of the work. Objectives are best planned by the worker and their supervisor together.

2. Review regularly

The supervisor and staff member should make regular checks together on how work is progressing. Use these sessions to identify problems and plan solutions. Solutions may include:

- Changing the **objectives**.
- Altering the **time-scale** of a project.
- Adjusting the **budget**.
- **Delegating** work to another person;
- Identifying gaps in skills or knowledge and planning **training** to remedy them.
- Organising **support** to overcome problems in the work.

3. Give positive feedback

Make sure staff and volunteers receive feedback on the positive aspects of their work. It is too easy to assume people know when they are doing a good job, and to say nothing. Everyone needs encouragement. Make feedback specific and focused on the work done, not on the person doing it – such as: *"That was a very effective project. I particularly liked the way you handled the avalanche of enquiries ...."* not *"You are a splendid person – keep up the good work"*.

4. Give constructive criticism

People can only improve their work if they know what needs to be improved. Make sure your organisation provides its workers with specific information about their work and ways in which it may be improved or changed.

Encourage a climate in which staff and volunteers expect to get feedback and to be self-critical, so that they can learn and develop their work.

Stages in managing poor performance

It is vital that staff and volunteers get the chance to put right any short-comings in their performance well before formal disciplinary processes are begun.

- Identify problems as early as possible. Discuss the problems in supervision sessions and agree action to overcome them. Be as specific as possible. Don't ignore problems and hope they will go away of their own accord.
- If the problems persist and performance still does not reach the agreed targets or standards, repeat the process. Note down in writing the exact areas in which improvements are required. Make sure that the person understands and agrees to the plans for improvements.
- If problems still persist, the supervisor may have to start disciplinary proceedings.

Standards of practice and discipline

Every organisation should have a code of practice for the behaviour and standards of performance of its staff and volunteers and procedures to deal with poor performance. It is extremely difficult to maintain a high standard of quality in the organisation's work if the organisation has not defined what it means by quality.

The code of practice divides in to two parts. The first covers behaviour which the organisation considers to be wholly unacceptable. Breaches of this code will lead to disciplinary action or even summary dismissal.

The second part of the code covers the standards that are expected of each staff member and volunteer in their work. These should be agreed with the people concerned and are usually specific to each particular job.

If your staff belong to a trade union then the union should normally be involved in agreeing the disciplinary procedure. The union also has a role to play during the procedure in acting on behalf of the person involved.

Disciplinary proceedings

The disciplinary process has two main purposes:

- To **reprimand** and ensure non recurrence
- To **dismiss** for gross misconduct.

If a staff member or volunteer persistently falls short of the agreed standards of performance for her or his job, then your organisation may have to employ a disciplinary procedure.

Disciplinary procedure may also be necessary if a person commits a **serious breach** of your organisation's code of practice. This includes acts of gross misconduct such as:

- Theft, fraud or dishonesty.
- Serious and dangerous breaches of safety rules.
- Working whilst under the influence of drugs.
- Offensive, racist or sexist behaviour;
- Vandalism.
- Seriously breaches of the rules of confidentiality.

- Bringing the organisation into disrepute.

The disciplinary procedure should be written down and set out exactly what will happen to the staff member. It must be fair and should conform to guidelines such as those produced by the Advisory, Conciliation and Arbitration Service (ACAS). Details are given in *Chapter 10*.

At each stage of the disciplinary process, make sure that all parties know:

- What is considered to be wrong?
- What must be done to put it right?
- The timetable for putting things right?
- Who will assess the improvements?
- What will happen if the improvements are not made?

Make sure your organisation has proper procedures for disciplinary matters. If all goes well you may never have to use them. However, it is very hard to take any action following a breach of discipline unless you have a process for doing so. Mistakes in the process can be very costly – the organisation may be taken to an Industrial Tribunal and, if it were to lose the case, could be required to pay compensation. In addition, the organisation is likely to suffer bad publicity and serious harm to morale if such matters are mishandled.

Unfair dismissal

An organisation should not dismiss staff unless they have first exhausted every other avenue to remedy the situation. Even then, your managing committee must see that the dismissal is fair.

This means that you must be able to prove to yourselves and to the rest of the staff team that the staff member:

- Is unwilling or unable to do the work for which she or he is hired.
- Or has committed gross misconduct.
- Or has continued to break the rules even after warnings.

Disciplinary Procedure

TECHNICAL DETAIL

Disciplinary proceedings usually have the following stages:

1. Verbal warning

A formal, oral warning is usually given following minor breaches of discipline, or after unsuccessfully trying, through supervision to remedy shortcomings in performance.

The formal warning is recorded in the files of the staff member concerned.

2. Written warning

If problems still persist, the staff member should receive a written warning about their behaviour. A copy of this should be kept in the files. A person must receive two written warnings before being dismissed for poor performance. Procedures for this are set out in employment legislation.

3. Disciplinary Hearing

If the staff member still fails to put things right, following the first written warning, or if she or he is thought to have committed a serious breach of discipline, she or he must attend a **disciplinary hearing**. In cases of **gross misconduct**, the proceedings start here.

Every organisation should have guidelines for the conduct of such hearings. The staff member is usually entitled to be accompanied by a Trade Union Official, or by another "friendly person" to act on their behalf.

The organisation is represented by a panel of the senior member of staff and usually at least one member of the managing committee.

The hearing examines both sides of the complaint. The disciplinary panel should tell the staff member their decision at the hearing and confirm it, in writing, immediately afterwards.

Results of the hearing range from:

- Action to remedy the situation and details of the date by which the action must be taken.
- Notice that further misconduct will result in further disciplinary action or dismissal.
- Suspension without pay for up to seven days.
- Demotion or transfer.
- Dismissal – if the facts show that the misconduct was so serious as to merit it.

4. Appeals

Staff members should be entitled to appeal following any disciplinary proceedings, if they feel they have been treated unfairly.

The appeal might be heard by the employment sub-committee, by the officers of the managing committee, by the Chair, or, in some cases by the full committee itself.

Managing poor performance

CHECK POINT

- Does your managing committee receive enough information on the performance of your staff and volunteers?
- Does the organisation have systems of supervision and appraisal which identify poor performance before it becomes a crisis?
- Is there a written disciplinary procedure?
- Is it widely known and understood?
- Is there a written grievance procedure?

The managing committee must also be able to show that a proper disciplinary procedure was followed.

Handling grievances

A grievance occurs when a person feels they have been treated unfairly or improperly. As the employer, the managing committee should see that the organisation has a proper procedure for grievances from staff or volunteers. Grievances are usually dealt with in the following sequence:

1. The person raises their grievance with their supervisor. (If the grievance is about their supervisor, she or he should go to the next stage.) The matter is discussed and, if possible, sorted out at this stage.

2. The person puts details of the grievance in writing to the Chief Executive or to the Chair of the managing committee (or the relevant sub-committee). A meeting is arranged to hear details of the grievance and to try to resolve the matter.

3. If the grievance is still not sorted out, the organisation may request help from an outside body, such as ACAS.

Communicating with staff

Much emphasis has been placed on trustees receiving information from members of the organisation who carry out the work – the staff and volunteers. The flow of information should not be one way. You and all the other trustees have a duty to make sure that the decisions that are made by the managing committee and the reasons for those decisions are communicated effectively to all members of the organisation. If this is not done, the trustee body is likely to become remote from the day to day work and will not be effective.

TECHNICAL DETAIL

Methods of communicating between the trustees and all the staff.

1 Through the Chief Executive

Hierarchical, a trickle down effect. Very often information doesn't trickle down.

2 In writing

Information is communicated direct to all staff. This could include minutes of meetings or a summary of the key points that effect staff. This may be practical in small organisations but may not be practical in large organisations. Staff may not read the information.

3 Briefing meetings

Following meetings of the managing committee, senior staff are briefed by Chief Executive, followed by each then briefing her or his staff team on the key decisions and their implications. This is a model that has been used very effectively in both public and private sectors. It requires setting aside time for short meetings that occur in a cascade throughout the organisation.

4 Ask all staff to attend the managing committee meetings

This is only an option in very small organisations.

5 Noticeboards

Notes of relevant decisions are displayed on noticeboards. This can be effective but only if staff are encouraged to read the boards.

Self-assessment

Working with paid staff

	Know	Must check
1. What are the main legal requirements you need to meet, as an employer?	☐	☐
2. What is the duty of care?	☐	☐
3. Can staff in voluntary organisations belong to a trade union?	☐	☐
4. What are the main parts of a staffing policy?	☐	☐
5. Why do you need to have job descriptions and person specifications?	☐	☐
6. What is staff development?	☐	☐
7. What are the eight main tasks of an employer?	☐	☐
8. In what ways can the managing committee supervise its senior staff member?	☐	☐
9. What are the main differences between the role of staff and that of the managing committee?	☐	☐
10. What difference does the management style make to an organisation?	☐	☐
11. What are the main steps in a disciplinary procedure?	☐	☐
12. On what grounds might a person be summarily dismissed?	☐	☐

Working with volunteers

NEED TO KNOW

Your responsibilities

Volunteers make a huge contribution to the life and work of many charities. In some respects they are treated in a similar way to paid employees, in others they are much more like private citizens. The trustees must make sure that everything that volunteers do in the name of the organisation helps it to achieve its objects.

Your TRUSTEE responsibilities are to see that:

- **The organisation *obeys the law* with respect to volunteers.**
- **The organisation discharges its *duty of care* towards volunteers, and to those with whom the volunteers work.**
- **Volunteers are *insured* as required by law.**

Your MANAGEMENT responsibilities are to make sure that:

- **The involvement of volunteers is properly thought out and *supervised*.**
- **Volunteers are *not misused or exploited*.**
- **You receive *information* on the activities of volunteers and the contribution they make to the organisation.**
- **Volunteers are given *recognition* for the work that they do.**

Keeping to the law

As a general rule, volunteers should be treated in a similar way to paid employees. Whilst volunteers are not the same as paid staff, they are entitled to the same level of care and consideration, supervision and fairness.

The managing committee should make sure the organisation takes account of the following matters that affect volunteers directly.

- **Welfare benefits:** Volunteers who are in receipt of welfare benefits must be aware of the regulations which affect what they can do, and the limits to what they can receive in expenses.

For more information see *"Effective Trustee, Part 2", page 42*.

- **Payments** to volunteers may be subject, in some circumstances, to income tax. Where payments cover only the cost of expenditure incurred by a volunteer, there will be no problem. If payments are made in lump sums, or as honoraria, the tax implications should be checked carefully. If payments are made for car mileage then this can attract income tax, above certain rates. (Contract the Volunteer Centre UK for details.)
- **Equal opportunities:** Equal opportunity legislation covers volunteers as well as paid staff, and equal opportunities policies should too. Volunteering should be open to all.
- **Health and Safety legislation:** This applies in the same way as to paid staff. Volunteers should be shown the health and safety policy, and agree to abide by

it. Volunteers should be properly trained in using equipment, and know what to do in the event of an accident. Failure by the organisation to provide adequate safety measures for volunteers could result in prosecution and a requirement to pay compensation.

- **Recruitment:** The processes used to recruit volunteers should be fair and make it possible to involve anyone who has appropriate skills and experience. The recruitment of volunteers is covered by the Race Relations Act, Sex Discrimination Act, and the Fair Employment Act (NI) for Nothern Ireland. Volunteers should not face discrimination on any unfair or irrelevant grounds.

- **Work with children:** Where volunteers work with children, the organisation should have a suitable code of practice. The Home Office has recently issued a recommended code of practice *"Safe from Home"*. This will ensure reasonable care is taken to protect vulnerable children. Voluntary organisations are *not* generally able to check on the police records of volunteers. This can be possible where volunteers work unsupervised for long periods of time with children. For more information, you should consult the Home Office Circular HOC 117/92.

- **Insurance:** Volunteers who drive their own vehicles on your organisation's behalf will need to be covered by their own insurance policy. This should be checked in writing. The organisation might consider taking out the following insurance for volunteers:

Protection of no-claims bonus. Protects volunteers against loss of their no-claims bonus as a result of the volunteer driving.

Personal accident insurance. Provides compensation in the event of injury or death.

Professional indemnity insurance. Where volunteers give advice to members of the public.

For more detail on the legal side of managing volunteers see *Book 14* in *Chapter 10.*

The duty of care

Your organisation has a duty to ensure that volunteers are treated and deployed with reasonable care, given the type of work they do. "Reasonable care" is a flexible concept – it is essentially what an ordinary person would regard as reasonable in a particular situation.

If volunteers are themselves vulnerable (i.e. more likely to be at risk) or are working with vulnerable people, the organisation has an enhanced duty of care.

The organisation could be liable to pay compensation if it is found by the courts not to have taken reasonable care to

Your duties towards volunteers

CHECK POINT

- Do you have a policy on volunteer involvement?
- Are volunteers recruited using effective procedures, so that neither they, nor the people they work with are put at unreasonable risk?
- Do you ensure that volunteers understand and follow your Health and Safety policy? Do volunteers agree to abide by the policy?
- Does your equal opportunities policy cover the involvement of volunteers? How is it implemented and monitored?
- Does each volunteer get a clear description of her or his job, and preparation on how to do it?
- Are your volunteers properly insured? When did you last check?
- Are you confident that the managing committee is discharging its duty of care to volunteers and your clients?

TECHNICAL DETAIL

A policy on volunteers

The main ingredients of a policy on volunteers includes:

- The Mission Statement of the organisation.
- The philosophy of volunteering in the organisation (including equality of opportunity to become a volunteer).
- The roles of volunteers.
- The relationship between volunteers and paid staff.
- The recruitment of volunteers.
- The support of volunteers.
- Meeting the costs of volunteer involvement (expenses, insurance, etc.).
- The training and personal development of volunteers.
- Monitoring the performance of volunteers.
- Ways of giving volunteers recognition and respect.
- A code of practice for volunteers.

prevent injury or damage. This could result in trustees being personally liable to cover the cost of compensation. See *Book 14* in *Chapter 10*.

Involving volunteers

You should think carefully about the way in which the organisation involves volunteers. You should consider producing a policy document or code of practice on volunteering. This will provide a framework for good working practice with volunteers.

This may seem unwieldy and bureaucratic. It should not be so. Volunteers are a vital and valuable resource for the organisation. They give their time and energy to help you to advance towards your aims. It is only fair that you manage them properly and provide them with a rewarding and worthwhile experience.

Volunteering is a two way process – volunteers give their time, energy and skills. In return, they get various non-monetary rewards. An effective organisation tries to identify the motivations of its volunteers and find appropriate ways of recompensing them for their commitment.

The responsibility for involving volunteers can be allocated to an individual or to a sub-committee. The detailed task of drawing up a code of practice or policy can then be delegated.

The effective involvement of volunteers requires thought and good management. It should not be left to chance. You and the other trustees are responsible for what volunteers do. You should see they have clear roles to play, are properly briefed and well looked after, have the necessary skills to do a good job, are supervised effectively and generally bring credit to the organisation. Some ideas for good volunteer involvement are given in the checklist on page 44.

Volunteers who work with vulnerable people

It is particularly important that volunteers are properly selected and supervised where they work with vulnerable people. There has been much debate about the best way to ensure the safety of vulnerable clients – especially children. Ultimately, the best protection is given by effective selection of volunteers and by making sure they are properly supervised.

Investing in your volunteers

Volunteers work for no financial gain, but to really benefit from their efforts most organisations will need to invest staff time and money in their volunteers. You should see that sufficient resources are allocated in the budget to recruit, select, supervise, train and organise the volunteers. No volunteer should be out of pocket as a result of their activities. Every volunteer should feel that their organisation really does believe in the unique contribution they make, recognise it and want it to grow and develop.

Looking after volunteers

- Does someone take responsibility to ensure that every volunteer is in regular contact and is supervised? If so, who?

- Do volunteers discuss their work with their supervisor (whether formally or informally) and plan new work?

- Do volunteers receive positive feedback on their work?

- Does the organisation as a whole recognise the contribution made by volunteers? And how is this done?

Code of Practice for Volunteers working with vulnerable people

1. Develop a policy on how to safeguard the people your organisation works with, in keeping with the values, aims and style of your organisation.

2. Agree procedures for staff and volunteers which prevent clients from being put at unreasonable risk. Supervision is essential to achieve this.

3. Make sure all volunteers have a clear role to play, and do not step outside the role without discussing it first.

4. Interview and select volunteers with proper care. Use structured interviews and application forms to find out relevant information about the volunteer. This can include asking about their past criminal record.

5. Take references on the volunteers you propose to take on.

6. Recruit the volunteers for an initial, supervised probationary period.

7. Make sure staff are prepared and trained to work with volunteers.

8. Make sure the organisation does not destroy the whole ethos of its volunteer involvement by introducing inappropriate rules and regulations. The managing committee must be sure that it is taking reasonable, sensible steps to ensure the safety of those with whom it works.

A 12-point checklist for volunteer involvement

1. Why does your organisation wish to involve volunteers? Are volunteers the best way to get the work done? What do volunteers bring to the work that is special or different?

2. Does each volunteer have a clear job to do? Are the jobs appropriate for volunteers? Do the jobs offer real satisfaction to volunteers?

3. Are volunteers recruited and deployed fairly? Do you have a commitment to equal opportunities for volunteers? How is it implemented? How is it monitored?

4. Do you have a proper system for recruitment, interview and selection of volunteers? Do you ensure that your organisation takes adequate steps to protect volunteers and clients from risk? Do you take references on volunteers, where they will be working with vulnerable people?

5. Is each volunteer given a description of the job she or he is expected to do? Are they informed of the terms and conditions under which they are working? Do you make sure each volunteer is properly briefed before they start work? Do they know what to do, where, when, how often, for how long, who to report to, etc.

6. Do volunteers have regular meetings with their co-ordinator or manager, to provide support, answer queries, supervise, identify and solve problems, and so on? Do volunteers work for a probationary or trial period before making a longer commitment?

7. Do you provide relevant training and development opportunities to enable volunteers to learn and grow in their work?

8. Does the organisation provide:
    *   Re-payment of out-of-pocket expenses?
    *   Insurance?
    *   Information on the organisation to keep the volunteer informed?
    *   Procedures for reporting back regularly on their work?
    *   Information on how volunteering will affect their welfare benefits (where appropriate)?

9. Can volunteers participate in planning and decision making that affects their work? How are their voices heard? Can volunteers appeal about decisions made that affect them? If so, how? Do you have disciplinary procedures for volunteers?

10. Do you review the way your organisation involves volunteers on a regular basis?

11. Do you have clear policies about the relationship between volunteers and paid staff?

12. Can volunteers assume greater responsibilities, or change jobs within the organisation? Do you enable volunteers to find new or alternative placements with other agencies?

ACTIVITY

Why volunteers remain committed

Read through the list below. Tick the four statements which you think are most important. Write down what your organisation actually does to make sure these four things happen.

Your volunteers:

☐ Feel appreciated.

☐ Have a sense of belonging and being part of a "team" among their co-workers.

☐ Can see their work **does** make a difference.

☐ Are involved in some of the decisions which affect their work, such as objective setting, problem solving, etc.

☐ Are given a chance for advancement.

☐ Are treated as working partners by paid staff.

☐ Are provided with an opportunity for personal growth.

☐ Feel that their personal needs are being met.

☐ Receive recognition from the organisation for their work.

Other *(please specify):*

☐ Feel capable of handling the tasks offered.

Self-assessment

Working with volunteers

	Know	Must check
1. What are the main legal considerations you need to be aware of when involving volunteers?	☐	☐
2. What steps can an organisation take to insure its volunteers?	☐	☐
3. What is the "duty of care" and how does it apply to volunteers?	☐	☐
4. Why should organisations develop a policy on volunteering?	☐	☐
5. What are the main points you should cover when you involve volunteers?	☐	☐
6. What steps should you take when volunteers work with vulnerable people?	☐	☐
7. What are the benefits of supervising volunteers?	☐	☐
8. In what ways can you supervise volunteers?	☐	☐
9. How do supervision needs vary over time?	☐	☐
10. What investment should you make to ensure high quality volunteers?	☐	☐

5

Chapter

Recruiting the people your organisation needs

NEED TO KNOW

Your responsibilities

The staff who carry out the work of your organisation are its most valuable asset. Make sure that your managing committee has thought out its approach to recruitment and selection so that you are able to get people with the right skills, experience and attitudes.

Your TRUSTEE responsibilities are to make sure that:

- Your organisation *obeys the law* regarding recruitment of staff.
- You recruit *fairly*, within an *equal opportunities* framework.

Your MANAGEMENT responsibilities are to see that:

- The organisation has *proper procedures* for the recruitment of staff and volunteers.
- Records are kept of applicants, so that the organisation can *monitor* the recruitment process.

This chapter focuses on the recruitment of paid staff. Many of the principles are similar when recruiting volunteers. However, there are some important differences. These are described at the end of the chapter.

Recruitment and the law

All organisations should aim to recruit **the best person for the job.** The managing committee should ensure that no applicant suffers discrimination on any unfair grounds not just on the grounds of sex or race, but equally on the grounds of disabilities that are unrelated to the job, or any other unrelated factor. This would not only be morally wrong but is ineffective recruiting practice.

You must see that the organisation obeys the law with regard to recruitment. The **Sex Discrimination Act 1975** and the **Race Relations Act 1976** together make it an offence to discriminate

directly or indirectly on the grounds of race, colour, ethnic origin, nationality, national origin, sex or marital status.

The only exception to this is where there are **genuine occupational qualifications** for a job. For example, an organisation may be allowed to recruit a woman worker to work with young girls in a residential setting. Otherwise, **any** discrimination on these grounds is unlawful. Organisations are not allowed to engage in positive discrimination, say, in favour of black applicants, even if black people are under-represented in the organisation. They are allowed to **encourage** applications from particular sections of the community, however.

47

The Race Relations Act does not cover Northern Ireland. A separate order extends the Sex Discrimination Act to Northern Ireland. In addition, organisations are required to obey the **Fair Employment (NI) Act 1989** which prohibits direct or indirect discrimination on the grounds of religion. All employers with 10 employees or more must monitor the religious make up of their workforce each year.

The Equal Pay Act 1970 requires that men and women receive equal pay for equivalent work or work of the same nature.

The Disabled Persons (Employment) Act 1944 requires that at least 3% of the workforce must be made up of registered disabled people, for employers of more than 20 people, unless an exemption is granted.

The Rehabilitation of Offenders Act 1974 entitles people not to reveal certain criminal convictions which are considered "spent" after a certain length of time. Employment in the social services field is usually exempt from the Act. This means candidates for a social service job **can** be asked to disclose all previous criminal convictions.

If you have any doubts about employment law, your organisation should check with its legal advisors.

The recruitment process

The guiding principles when recruiting staff are to be clear exactly what the person is expected to so, and to select people with the skills and experience to be able to do it.

The process has the following ten stages:

1. **Job analysis:** checking what work needs to be done.
2. **Job description:** setting out in writing exactly what the job involves.
3. **Person specification:** setting out the skills, knowledge, experience and other qualities which are essential to do the job.

   The selection process can then be focused on the essential components of the person specification.
4. **Producing an application form:** designing a form to gather information from job applicants.
5. **Producing an information pack:** putting together relevant information for applicants, about the job and the organisation.
6. **Advertising for the job:** drafting the advertisement and placing it in suitable publications, with recruitment and employment agencies, etc.
7. **Receiving responses:** from the advertisement up to the closing date.
8. **Short-listing:** selecting a short list of applicants for interview.
9. **Interviewing:** interviewing applicants to select the best person for the job.
10. **Selection:** taking up references, prior to confirming the appointment.

Members of the managing committee will be closely involved in the recruitment of senior staff in larger organisations. In smaller organisations the committee may be involved in all appointments.

The actual task of recruitment is best delegated to a sub-committee. The managing committee as a whole should establish clear guidelines for the process. This can be covered in your organisation's staffing policy, or there could be a separate recruitment policy.

Job descriptions and person specifications

Every member of staff should have a written description of their job that is accurate, achievable and focuses on the results of their work, not just on the process of doing it.

The **Job Description** should list:

- **Hours** to be worked.
- **Location** of the job.
- **Salary** – actual salary or salary range offered.
- **Lines of accountability** – who is the job-holder responsible to?
- The **tasks** the job-holder is expected to perform.
- The main **results** expected from carrying out the job (in terms of both quality and quantity).
- **Terms and conditions** of employment.

The **person specification** will list the criteria that are considered **essential** to carry out the job:

- **Skills, knowledge and attitudes** that are essential and desirable.
- Any **qualifications** that are required.
- Any **personal qualities** or attributes, such as willingness to work in a team or alone.
- Any **personal circumstances**, such as being able to travel to work, or work in the evenings.

The person specification enables the selection panel to concentrate on finding evidence that candidates fulfil criteria that are essential to the job.

When you are recruiting a new person for the job, you should look only for those skills which are necessary for the job. This helps to ensure a fair process of selection. Using unrelated, irrelevant criteria (such as gender or race) is bad practice and may be illegal.

Advertising the vacancy

The managing committee should check that appropriate methods are used to advertise job vacancies. For part-time and clerical posts, you may decide to use local papers. For more senior, full-time posts, it is advisable to widen the net and to make use of the national or specialist press.

The cost of recruitment

Remember to take into account the cost of recruitment. Newspapers and journals are, understandably, keen for you to take as large an advertising space as they can sell you (*and* for several weeks!). The size of the advertisement should relate to the importance and status of the job and to the resources available to your organisation.

The most important factor is to have an advertisement that is large enough to contain all the relevant information. Costs can be kept low by taking a minimum amount of space.

Other costs in recruitment include re-imbursement of the travel and subsistence costs of people attending interviews; postage and printing (which can be substantial if large numbers of people apply); re-location expenses of new staff members (if you offer this). Your organisation should make sure it has allowed for these costs in its budgets.

Job advertisements are also an important promotional tool for the organisation. They are read quite widely. Make sure your advertising gives the messages you want to give about your organisation. Does it seem to be a confident, lively organisation? Does it seem old-fashioned and cliquey?

Short-listing and interviewing

The managing committee should see that written guidance is produced for the selection panel for both the interview and selection processes. People can benefit from training in interview and selection. Your committee could have the long-term aim of offering training to those of its members who will take part in the selection process.

The managing committee will usually set up a **panel** for short-listing and interviewing for full time posts. It usually involves, as a minimum, two members of

49

ACTIVITY

Methods of recruitment

Effective recruitment must attract people who have the skills and qualities needed to do the job well. Your organisation should aim to attract a good field of applicants for each vacancy. To do this you will need to attract the interest of a wide range of people. You can employ a variety of recruitment methods to do this.

First of all you should offer a chance to apply for the vacancy to your existing members of staff. This is particularly important where staff are on short term contracts or face redundancy. If the vacancy cannot be adequately filled from within your organisation, you must recruit from outside.

The main methods of recruitment:

Word of mouth: often very effective but may reach a very limited pool of people. If you plan to use word-of-mouth methods, make sure you combine this with other approaches.

Local press: reaches people in the local area. More suitable for part-time and non-professional jobs.

National press: reaches a wide audience. The most popular paper for charity appointments is the Guardian (Mondays and Wednesdays). The other quality papers reach different audiences.

Job centres: a free service, but may have limited relevance for skilled, professional posts.

Mailings: make use of other organisations' mailings or in-house magazines. These can reach targeted audiences such as artists, disabled people, etc.

Trade journals: reach particular professional groups such as accountants, social workers, personnel specialists.

Specialist press: reaches particular sections of the community – such as the *Asian Times*, and the *Voice*.

Agencies and consultants: More charities are now using agencies to help them to recruit their staff. This applies mostly to senior staff posts. It can be costly, and your organisation must be able to rely on the professional skills and judgement of the agency concerned.

Activity

Read through the list of recruitment methods. Identify which your organisation uses for which types of vacancy. Find out whether the effectiveness of the different methods it uses is monitored. Hold a discussion at a committee meeting on how recruitment methods might be improved.

the committee, plus the senior staff member. Other people may be brought in for, for example, their expertise. Sometimes an outsider is used, with a different perspective on the organisation and its work.

Selection panels should be reasonably balanced (over time) by gender, race, age and disability. It is not usually possible to create a perfectly representative single panel, without making the panel so large that it becomes ineffective.

The **short-listing** process involves each panel member reading through each application form and giving each applicant a score for each of the **essential** criteria in the person specification. The panel members agree the six to eight applicants who best meet the person specification. These are invited to attend an interview. The panel will also conduct the **interviews**. A member of the managing committee should chair the panel. The interview questions should be agreed in advance, and allocated to the panel members.

Make sure that:

- The questions are **job-related**.
- The questions are **fair**.
- All candidates are asked the **same** basic questions.
- A written **record** is kept of each candidate's answers. This is vital in case any candidate raises objections to the way the interviews are conducted.
- All members of the panel use an agreed system for **rating** the candidates. This usually involves giving a score for each of the essential criteria in the person specification.

Once the interviews are over, make sure that:

- Each candidate is **informed** in writing of the decision.
- The successful candidate is **invited** to take up the appointment, subject to her or his **references** being satisfactory.

TECHNICAL DETAIL

The Job Advertisement

The following information should appear in the job advert:

- The job title
- A brief description of the job
- A brief description of the essential and desirable requirements
- The salary and salary scales
- Whether the post is full-time, temporary, part-time, etc.
- The name and address of organisation
- The contact telephone number for informal enquiries
- The closing date – at least three weeks after the advert's publication
- A statement about equal opportunities

Take particular care with the wording of the advertisement – write in plain English, use words that are understandable, avoid jargon and abbreviations.

Interviews should be a two-way process in which your organisation finds out about the applicants and they find out about your organisation. Good interviews draw out the best from all the applicants and should leave them feeling that they were given a fair chance, even if they were not successful.

For more on interviewing see *Book 17* in *Chapter 10*.

The timetable for recruitment

Recruiting staff takes time. The process must be properly planned and everyone in the organisation should be aware of the date for each stage.

Job analysis, writing the job description and person specification should all be done before the previous postholder has left.

The job advertisement takes time to place with the press. If you plan to use a monthly journal it may take five weeks or more to place the advert. You need to have all the information for applicants, about the job and the organisation, ready for the date of the advert. The advert should spell out deadlines for receipt of applications which will normally be 2-3 weeks after the advertisement last appears.

Applicants should be told the date of interviews. These are usually about one month after the advert date to allow time for shortlisting. There may be a delay of some months between appointment of a new staff member and their starting date while the notice period in their previous job is worked.

Induction

Make sure that all new staff are properly introduced to their jobs, to the organis-ation, and to other staff and volunteers. Good induction helps new staff to settle in quickly, identifies areas in which any extra help or support is needed and ensures that staff have a clear picture of what they are expected to do.

It is helpful to develop a basic induction procedure which includes an information pack for all new staff. This can be easily adapted to fit the requirements of different staff.

Recruiting volunteers

The managing committee should make sure that the organisation has suitable procedures for recruiting volunteers. Recruitment of volunteers is a less formal process than that used for paid staff. Your organisation needs to be sure that it has:

- Work which it is appropriate for volunteers to do.
- A proper system for meeting and interviewing volunteers and matching them to the tasks that need doing.
- Allocated the time of a member of staff or the committee to support each volunteer.

Reaching volunteers

Volunteers can be reached through a variety of channels. Surveys have consistently shown that word or mouth – being asked by a committee member or member of staff or another volunteer – is the most effective way to recruit volunteers. Don't rely on casual word of mouth. Get people from your organisation to go out and spread the word. Target your word of mouth campaign so that you reach people you otherwise tend to miss.

Recruiting staff

- Is there an adequate job description?
- Has your organisation produced a person specification?
- Has your organisation identified the attributes that are essential for the job?
- Where and how will the vacancy be advertised?
- Is your application form adequate and geared to finding out about the essential attributes for the job?
- Who will shortlist applications and interview the applicants?
- Does the interview panel understand equal opportunities?
- Is a record kept of all the questions and answers at the interviews?
- Does your organisation provide induction for new staff?

CHECK POINT

Example
Spreading the word

The managing committee of Centre 88 – a drop-in for people in mental distress – decided to recruit new volunteer counsellors. Each committee member agreed to give time to contacting one organisation or network to talk to people about the opportunities. They produced the following list of "targets".

- The local evangelical church.
- The local mosque.
- The Sikh Temple.
- A pre-retirement course run by a major employer.
- The trades council.
- The local job-club.
- The Diocesan Board for Social Responsibility.
- The University Students Union.
- A local community centre.

Interviewing volunteers

Your organisation should use interview processes that are appropriate to the work the volunteers will do. If volunteers are doing simple administrative and fundraising tasks, then the interview may be quite informal. If volunteers are involved in working with vulnerable people or undertaking work which requires particular skills, or they will be representing the organisation in public, then the interviews will need to be more rigorous.

The interview is a two-way process:

Volunteers need to find out:

- Exactly what is **expected of them**.
- Whether the job appeals and **suits** them.
- How much **time** is involved.
- About the **organisation**.
- Whether **training** is required.
- Whether **expenses** are provided.

Methods of reaching potential volunteers

TECHNICAL DETAIL

Posters.

Leaflets.

Exhibitions and displays.

Talks to schools, community centres, employers, religious organisations, clubs, societies – anywhere where people can be found.

Pre-retirement courses.

Local radio.

Local press – news stories, features and adverts.

Local free newspapers.

National press (for national charities).

Public service announcements on independent television.

Television.

Teletext.

The mailings and newsletters sent out by other organisations.

Magazines and journals.

Your own organisation's newsletters.

Word of mouth.

You can also use the local **Volunteer Bureau** and other **organisations which help people to find voluntary work.** Look up the number in your phone book or contact the organisations listed in *Chapter 10.*

The organisation needs to find out:

- What the volunteer **can** do.
- What the volunteer **wants** to do.
- Relevant **experience**.
- Relevant **skills** and **knowledge**.
- Relevant **details** – name, address, telephone number, etc.
- **Availability**.
- Other **information** relevant to the work.
- Whether the volunteer has any **special needs.**

Volunteer recruitment

CHECK POINT

Why does your organisation want to recruit volunteers?
- What will volunteers do?
- Is involving volunteers the best way to achieve the results?
- Has your organisation produced a list of the tasks that the volunteers will do?
- How many volunteers are needed? When?
- What skills, experience, knowledge, or attitudes must the volunteers have?

What information does your organisation have on the local population from which you are recruiting?
- What is the size of the population, how is it made up?
- What are the interests and concerns of particular groups in the population? Are they relevant to your organisation?

What messages does your organisation give about itself, its need for volunteers and how volunteers will benefit from being involved?

What methods of recruitment does your organisation use?
- Have you reviewed all available methods?
- What methods have worked best in the past?

Has your organisation drawn up a volunteer recruiting plan?
- When will it recruit? Over what time span?
- How will it recruit? Who will do the work?
- How will new volunteers be received? When will they be interviewed?
- Will they be prepared or trained before they start?
- How will they be supported?

What resources are needed for recruiting volunteers? Are they included in the budget?

- For certain types of volunteer work (with children, for example) whether the volunteer has any **criminal convictions** which might affect their involvement.

The ideal involvement of volunteers leads to a balance between volunteer giving time and effort to the organisation and getting something back for themselves (such as sense of achievement, helping people, meeting new people, learning new skills).

Remember that the trustees have a duty of care towards both volunteers and the people with whom they work. You must be seen to be taking reasonable steps to ensure that volunteers are appropriately selected and managed.

Induction for volunteers

Make sure that your organisation provides an appropriate level of induction for your volunteers. This might range from a short introductory chat through to a detailed induction process, much like that for paid staff. Good induction will help the volunteers to settle in to their work and ensures they know what is expected of them.

Self-assessment

Recruiting the people your organisation needs

	Know	Must check

1. What is prohibited under anti-discrimination legislation? ☐ ☐

2. What other legislation should employers be aware of when recruiting? ☐ ☐

3. Why is the job description so important? ☐ ☐

4. What is a person specification? ☐ ☐

5. What are the main methods of recruiting staff? ☐ ☐

6. What are "essential criteria" when shortlisting applicants for a vacancy? ☐ ☐

7. How can an organisation keep its advertising and recruitment costs down? ☐ ☐

8. What are the main considerations to bear in mind when interviewing applicants for a vacancy? ☐ ☐

9. What are the main methods for reaching potential volunteers? ☐ ☐

10. What information must an organisation find out about its volunteers? ☐ ☐

Managing premises

NEED TO KNOW

Your responsibilities

The managing committee is responsible for making sure that any premises owned or leased (other than property held purely for investment purposes) are helping the organisation to achieve its objectives and purposes.

Your TRUSTEE responsibilities are to see that your premises are:

- **Owned or leased *under the control* of the trustees, and to know the terms of the lease (rent and rate review periods, responsibilities regarding repairs and dilapidation).**
- **Properly *insured*.**
- ***Safe* and *healthy*.**
- **Well maintained and kept in *good condition* so that the value is maintained.**
- **Properly *valued* in the accounts.**
- ***Give a reasonable return* if owned by the organisation and leased to other agencies or hired out to users.**

You must also ensure that your organisation:

- **Receives the mandatory 80% *rate relief* from the local rating authority, available only if you are a charity.**
- **Obeys the 1971 Town and County Planning Act and any other *regulations* affecting your buildings.**

Your MANAGEMENT responsibilities are to ensure that the premises are:

- ***Well managed*, clean and reflect the ethos and values of the organisation.**
- **Used to *capacity*.**
- **Kept in a *good state* of decoration and repair.**

The premises you occupy

If your organisation already occupies premises, you need to know whose name is on the lease or freehold. If your organisation is **not incorporated**, then two or more people will be signatories to the freehold or lease, on behalf of the organisation. These people are holding trustees. If this is the case, the committee

members will normally be personally responsible for seeing that the terms of the lease are met and that rent is paid. It is possible to draw up a lease which specifically excludes the committee from any personal liability. If the organisation is **incorporated**, it can hold property in its own name and any liabilities will not be the responsibility of committee members unless a guarantee is given.

If you **lease property** you should:

- Understand your personal responsibilities and **liabilities** under the lease, even if your organisation is incorporated.
- Check the **terms of the lease**.
- Make sure you abide by the lease agreement – in particular, make sure that the **rent is paid** on the due date and check your obligations for **repairs**.
- Find out when the rent is **reviewed** and make sure you budget for any increases as a result of a rent review.
- Find out whether you can make **alterations** to the building and whether you have to meet their full cost.
- Check what right you have to **renew** the lease when the current agreement terminates.
- Check the terms for **surrendering the lease**. Will you have to pay rent for the whole period even if you have to surrender early? The sudden loss of funding from a project could easily cause this to happen.
- Make sure you abide by any restrictions on **use of the premises** set out in the lease. This can include the hours in which the building may be used, limits on certain activities, etc.
- Plan well ahead for the time when the **lease ends**. Will you be able to stay? If not, where will you move to?

An alternative to leasing is to purchase the building which you intend to occupy. This can be done using a mortgage from a bank or building society, or through a payment from reserves or by mounting a fundraising appeal. The advantages of owning a building are that the organisation has a long-term asset, the value of which will usually grow. The costs of occupying the building will diminish rather than increase over time. You are free to use the building to suit your requirements, as long as you obey the law and local by-laws. However, your organisation is

responsible for every aspect of the building. You are also more tied down to the building, should you need to expand or move.

If your organisation owns the premises it occupies, the trustees should check that the building is in:

- Sound **condition**, structurally. Is it inspected regularly?
- A good state of **repair**, inside and out.
- Good **decorative order**.

You should also see that money is set aside each year for future repairs or renewals of a substantial nature. For example, replacing old windows, repairing boundary walls. This is called "making a provision" in the accounts". Finally the trustees should make sure that the building is revalued form time to time, so that its worth as an asset is accurately reflected in the accounts.

Whether your organisation **owns** its own building, or leases premises, the managing committee should see that:

- The premises are **well used**. It is a waste of the charity's money to have buildings standing idle.
- The premises are **safe and healthy** in accordance with the 1963 Offices, Shops and Railway Premises Act.

If your organisation owns the premises that it occupies, the committee should check that:

- Your organisation abides by the planning regulations laid down in the Town and County Planning Acts. This means checking what you are allowed to **use** the building for, particularly if you are planning new uses, such as opening a charity shop. The regulations also limit what you can do to the outside and inside of buildings. This is especially true if your building is **listed** or is in a **conservation area**. Any new building will need planning permission.

57

TECHNICAL DETAIL

Health and safety regulations

The main health and safety regulations for premises are:

Fire Precautions: There must be adequate means of escape, access for fire fighters, fire fighting equipment and fire alarms.

The local authority and the fire brigade enforce these regulations. Always consult them before making any alterations to your premises.

First aid: You must provide a first aid box with dressings, bandages, etc., and basic first aid instructions.

Temperature: Rooms must be warm enough to work in. In offices this usually means a temperature of 16 degrees Celsius after the first hour of work.

Space per person: Each person should have a minimum of 40 square feet of floor space (roughly a square 6 feet 6 inches wide). Usually each person will occupy more than this.

Ventilation and lighting: Rooms must be properly lit and have reasonable air supply.

Toilets: You must provide toilets, hot and cold water, and space for hanging clothes. If there are more than five staff of different gender, you must provide separate facilities for each sex.

Water and food: You must provide clean drinking water and if people eat food on the premises, they must have a suitable place to do so.

Cleanliness: You must keep premises clean. Floors and stairs should be maintained properly and cleaned weekly. Rubbish should not be allowed to build up.

The occupier of premises is responsible for meeting these requirements. They are enforced by the **Environmental Health Department** of the local authority.

PRACTICAL INFORMATION

Nightmares of ownership

Organisations which own their premises can face major problems such as:

• Repairs ruin the organisation

Huge bills for structural repairs: the great menace is **dry rot and damp** in older buildings or **subsidence**. Bills for treatment or repairs can run in to tens of thousands of pounds. Not all organi-sations have the reserves to cover this.

• The building runs the organisation

Some organisations find all their energy goes in to keeping the building going, and they lose sight of their real purposes.

• Can't sell, can't move

Organisations may be unable to sell their buildings, and get stuck with unsuitable premises.

- Relevant planning permission is sought from the local planning authority for alterations or the erection of new buildings.
- The premises are **accessible** to people with impaired mobility, such as wheelchair users or elderly infirm clients. The 1970 Chronically Sick and Disabled Persons Act requires occupiers of premises to make **reasonable and practical provision** for access to the premises, access within the premises, parking and disabled toilet facilities.

Running your premises

The managing committee as a whole will not have the time to oversee the detailed running of the premises. This task is usually delegated to a sub-committee (such as the Finance and General Purposes Committee or a Premises Committee) or to a suitable member of staff. As a committee member, make sure you are confident that the building is being properly managed. This can be done by:

- Receiving an **annual report** on the premises, the health and safety record, access, and insurance.
- Making a **periodic inspection** of the premises for yourself.

Make your premises work for you

Your premises should reflect the values and ethos of your organisation. The premises themselves send messages to people about the organisation. Make sure your premises give the messages you want. Consider the following:

- How big do they need to be?
- What sort of equipment and furniture should you have?
- Do you need meeting space, training rooms, etc?
- How seriously does your organisation tackle access for disabled people?
- Where should your buildings be located?

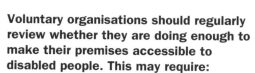

Make your buildings accessible

Voluntary organisations should regularly review whether they are doing enough to make their premises accessible to disabled people. This may require:

- **Widening doors.**
- **Building ramps or providing lifts.**
- **Providing adapted toilets.**
- **Adapting furniture and fittings to enable better access.**

Seek advice from disabled people and organisations of disabled people on access.

PRACTICAL POINTER

Running your premises

CHECK POINT

- Do you own or lease your premises?
- If you lease premises, have you checked the lease?
- When does it expire? When are rents due for re-negotiation?
- What are the organisation's liabilities for repairs, etc.?
- What plans do you have for new premises when the lease expires?
- Are your premises adequate for your organisation's needs?
- Are they well located?
- Do they give the right message about the organisation to users, and visitors?
- If you own your premises, have you had them revalued recently? Have they been surveyed or inspected to check they are structurally sound?
- Are your premises in good decorative order?
- Do you set aside money each year for renewals and repairs?
- If you hire out rooms, do you get a reasonable return or are you happy to provide a subsidy?
- Are the premises used fully and effectively to meet the aims and objectives of the organisation?
- Are the premises accessible to disabled people?

- What are the needs of staff and other users?
- How much can you reasonably afford to pay for your premises?
- What sort of decor is appropriate (colours, furniture, furnishings)?
- Are the premises kept in good decorative order?

Involving users in the premises

Ideas for improvements, better co-operation and improved working relationships between users can all be encouraged by involving users in decisions about the building. This can be done through staff meetings, if staff are the only users. If you use the premises for your work, then you can ask your customers and beneficiaries. If you let out some of your premises to other users, or hire out space to groups, you might want to consider setting up a users' sub-committee to advise the trustees on the use of the building. For more on running your premises, see *Books 18 and 19* in *Chapter 10*.

ACTIVITY

Assessing your premises

Visit your organisation's premises. What do you think about them? Are they right for your organisation? Why? If not, what should be changed?

Self-assessment

Managing your premises

	Know	Must check
1. What should trustees be particularly aware of, if the property is leased?	☐	☐
2. Who is responsible for the organisation's premises?	☐	☐
3. What are the main advantages of owning a building?	☐	☐
4. What are the main hazards of owning your own premises?	☐	☐
5. What are the main health and safety requirements for your premises?	☐	☐
6. What action should organisations take to ensure their buildings are accessible to disabled people?	☐	☐
7. What can be done to make sure your premises work effectively for your organisation?	☐	☐
8. How can you involve users in running your premises?	☐	☐

Working with members and users

NEED TO KNOW

Your responsibilities

As a trustee you are responsible for seeing that your managing committee establishes and keeps good links with the various people who have an interest in your activities (these are known as your stakeholders). This chapter looks at ways to make the links work, so as to build up collaboration and partnerships.

Your **TRUSTEE** responsibilities are to make sure that:

- The organisation *keeps in contact* with its membership according to the requirements of the governing instrument (this applies only to organisations with members).

- The managing committee *reports* to the people with an interest in the organisation as required by law or through funding and contractual agreements. *(See "The Effective Trustee, Part 2 for details of this.)*

Your **MANAGEMENT** responsibilities are to see that your organisation:

- Has a *planned approach* to keeping in contact with its membership.

- Works in ways that lead to *collaboration and partnership* with other agencies and organisations.

- Builds *good links* to the local and specialist communities it serves, through the local, national and specialist media.

- Keeps in *close contact* with the people for whom the charity is working, so as to understand their real needs and best meet them.

Links with your members

If your organisation has members (check this by looking in your governing instrument) the managing committee will usually be elected by the members at the Annual General Meeting. This means that the managing committee is itself a vital link with the wider membership. It also means that the AGM is a most important annual event to link the organisation to its members. Does your organisation make good use of its AGM?

In some organisations the supporters are called members, but have no formal position in the organisation's structure or right to take part in formal meetings.

In many voluntary organisations, little attention is paid to developing active, lively links with the membership. Your managing committee should see that the organisation has plans each year to:

- Keep members **informed** about the organisation.

PRACTICAL INFORMATION

Ways to build links with your members

- Produce a lively annual report.
- Involve members in open meetings, forums, seminars and so on, on matters of interest to them.
- Provide members with benefits, such as discounts for your publications or training courses that your organisation runs.
- Send members a newsletter or mailing on a regular basis, to keep them informed.
- Keep in touch through visits and telephone calls by staff, volunteers or trustees. Keep a record of when each person was last contacted.
- Invite members to events run by the organisation.

The same techniques can be used to keep contact with your supporters.

- Explain the **advantages** of being a member.
- Encourage **participation** in relevant meetings, events and the AGM.
- Attract and **involve** new members.
- Make sure that members pay **subscriptions**, if they are required to do so.
- See that there is an **up-to-date list** of members.

Your plans should pay attention to different types of member. Organisations may have individual members, member organisations, associate members, junior members and so on.

Election of the committee

Your organisation's governing instrument will lay down procedures for how the membership should elect the committee. Take steps to encourage people to stand for election. Breathe life into the process by circulating short CVs of the candidates, holding meetings to meet the candidates and encouraging a wide range of people to stand for election.

If your organisation has a **federal structure** make sure that the relationship between the local organisations and their regional or national body is clear. If local or regional groups elect representatives to be trustees, make sure they understand the role of a trustee *(see "The Effective Trustee, Part 1")*. When you are serving as a trustee you must **act independently and in the best interests of the charity** itself. You are not on the managing committee to represent the interests of others.

Building links to local authorities and other official bodies

Most charities are expected to collaborate with public services, provided this is in the best interests of their beneficiaries. The trustees should see that the organisation establishes good working links.

Avoid the temptation to build links to important official bodies (such as key funders) by asking each one to send an observer to your managing committee. This is not the most effective way to build good links. It can lead to confusion and clog up your committee with non-voting observers.

Instead, identify the reasons for building a link. Decide:

- The best level at which to establish the link (trustee; senior staff; working group; sub-committee).
- The best method to achieve the link (regular meetings; ad hoc meetings; one-to-one meetings, small group meetings).

Make sure that your organisation has considered how it links up with official bodies and for what purpose, and that it has planned an effective way to achieve these links.

Links with other charities

Charities which work in the same field have a duty to seek to collaborate with each other where possible, unless it is in the interests of their beneficiaries to compete. The same arguments for the approach to building links apply as for official bodies. Make sure your organisation uses methods which are effective in achieving collaboration.

Links with the public

All organisations need to attract support from the public. This helps to attract funding, donations, volunteer helpers and new members. The committee should take steps to ensure that the organisation makes itself known and keeps people informed about its activities. Your organisation should have a **public relations plan**. This need not be very elaborate, but you should make sure that you send out clear messages to the public about your organisation.

The committee should consider the publicity and public relations aspects of each of the main areas of your organisation's work, events and so on. Look out for opportunities to get your message across and get noticed. In smaller organisations, a member of the committee is often given special responsibility for public relations. In organisations with many paid staff, the work is usually given to a member of staff (such as a Press Officer, Public Relations Officer or Promotions Officer).

The committee should see that there is a healthy balance between the time and effort put into publicising and promoting the organisation and the time given to the work itself. Your organisation should be judged on the quality and quantity of services it provides to the people you serve (the beneficiaries) not by how well it promotes itself.

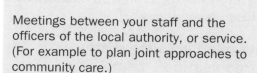

Ways to link with local authority and other official bodies

Meetings between your staff and the officers of the local authority, or service. (For example to plan joint approaches to community care.)

Involving members of public services in sub-groups of the managing committee, such as working groups on specific topics or sub-committees.

Meetings between trustees and elected members of the local authority.

Joint consultative committees.

Joint planning committees.

Strategy groups.

Informal visits by members of the local authority.

Regular monitoring visits.

Meetings to review the progress of the organisation.

Open days.

Seminars on the work of the organisation.

Regular bulletins on the work of the organisation.

Sending copies of the annual report.

PRACTICAL INFORMATION

Keeping in touch with your community

The trustees should see that the organisation has plans for keeping it in contact with the community with which it works. This may be the local community or it may be a particular community of people interested in your work.

These communities contain your actual and future supporters. It will pay your organisation to try to cultivate healthy interest. This means making positive use of methods of communicating with these communities.

Keeping in touch with your organisation's users

Many organisations seem to overlook the views of their users or clients. This is a serious mistake as it distances the organisation from the very people whose needs the organisation is supposed to be meeting. The trustees should make sure that they are satisfied that the organisation makes a real effort to keep in touch with the views and thereby needs of its users.

Your organisation could use a variety of methods to gather this information:

- An **annual survey** of views.
- Encourage **regular feedback** to staff and volunteers.
- Hold **open meetings** with users.
- Produce a **users newsletter**.
- Hold **question and answer** sessions with users.
- Hold a "meet the trustees" **evening**.
- Set up a **users committee** or forum.
- **Involve advocates** to work with users to enable them to contribute their views (for example where users are people with learning disabilities).

ACTIVITY

Some methods of keeping in touch

☐ Local and national press, features, news, photographs.

☐ Leaflets.

☐ Open days.

☐ Fun days.

☐ Open meetings and forums.

☐ Word of mouth.

☐ Surveys of users of services, public attitudes and awareness, etc.

☐ Local radio.

☐ The local library.

☐ Displays in the shops, banks building societies, etc.

☐ Parades.

☐ Campaigns.

☐ Television – news, features, in drama and soap operas, by using public service announcements, advertising.

☐ Car stickers.

☐ Direct mail.

☐ Badges/posters/billboards.

☐ Festivals.

☐ Award schemes.

Others *(please specify):*

Tick the methods your organisation uses to keep it in touch with the community it serves? What other methods do you use? Which are most effective? How do you know?

CHECK POINT

- Does your organisation have a membership?
- Is a variety of methods planned to keep the organisation in touch with its members?
- How does your organisation make links with public authorities such as your funders or public services?
- Does your organisation have collaborative links with other charities? How are these maintained?
- Has your organisation got a public relations plan?
- How does your organisation keep in touch with the community it serves?
- In what ways are your organisation's users involved with the organisation?

Self-assessment

Working with members and users

		Know	Must check
1.	What are four of the ways in which an organisation can maintain links with its members?	☐	☐
2.	What must representative trustees remember to do?	☐	☐
3.	In what circumstances must a charity collaborate with public agencies and other charities?	☐	☐
4.	What are the dangers of inviting public bodies to serve as observers on your managing committee?	☐	☐
5.	What are the benefits of effective public relations?	☐	☐
6.	What can an organisation do to keep in touch with the community it serves?	☐	☐
7.	What methods can an organisation use to maintain contact with its users?	☐	☐

Dealing with problems

NEED TO KNOW

Your responsibilities

The managing committee is responsible for making sure that problems are avoided, wherever possible, through good planning and by monitoring progress. You should be alert to early warning signs and ready to decide on appropriate action to deal with them.

Your TRUSTEE responsibilities are to see that you are properly informed about the progress the organisation is making and are alert to any problems that arise.

Your MANAGEMENT responsibility is to make sure that your organisation has clear and effective systems for dealing with crises or conflict.

What sorts of problems?

Voluntary organisations face a wide variety of problems. Some seem to live for the buzz of a good crisis. Effective organisations work hard to avoid crises as far as possible. However, even with the best management, occasional crises will still occur. Financial crisis is covered in *"The Effective Trustee, Part 2"*. In this chapter we focus on dealing with **organisational** problems:

- Managing conflict and disagreement.
- Reviving a flagging organisation.
- Involving outside consultants.

Staffing problems such as managing poor performance, grievance and disciplinary matters have been covered in *Chapter 3*.

Handling conflict

Conflict is a natural part of organisational life. Sooner or later, most organisations will encounter it. Conflict arises from differences of outlook between people. Too many committees adopt an ostrich-like approach to conflict – burying their heads in the sand and hoping it will just go away. In organisations, conflict most often arises because of:

- Differences of perception, opinion or beliefs about

  Power and authority – who's in control.

  The vision, aims and priorities of the organisation.

- Perceptions that there has been **unfair treatment** of some people in the organisation.

Or because of:

- Poor or **inadequate procedures** and systems so that people feel badly managed, unfairly treated, unclear about what is going on.
- **Inadequate resources** to do the work, so that people feel pressurised and undervalued.

Or because of **unresolved conflict** that simmers on from the past, hidden agendas, clashes of personality and so on.

An organisation is made up of various individuals. Each has their own unique view of the world. The organisation relies on trust, honesty and respect between its people. Problems begin to escalate towards conflict when the people concerned stop listening to each other, and then lose trust and respect. All parties can rapidly and easily descend in to a cycle of accusation and blame.

Ground rules for conflict resolution

Your organisation should establish some basic guidelines or ground rules for resolving conflict. This helps to reassure all concerned that their voices will be heard and that the organisation will seek a fair solution to the problems.

- Each person should be heard and allowed to explain their side of the matter.
- Discussion should focus on specific facts, events and incidents rather than on speculation and hearsay.
- Avoid attributing personal motives, or making personal attacks on the other parties.
- The process should seek to identify common ground and common interests.
- Encourage all parties to search for a solution that is in the interests of the organisation.
- A neutral or disinterested person from outside the organisation should be involved if the organisation cannot deal with the conflict in-house.

Using an outside person to help resolve conflict

Conflict is often very difficult to resolve from within an organisation, as everyone is too close to the issues. It can be helpful to bring in an outside person to enable you to resolve the conflict. This might be a **consultant,** a person from **ACAS**; a suitable **member of another organisation**. It is essential that the person is acceptable to all parties in the conflict. She or he must be fair and have no allegiance to one side over another.

PRACTICAL INFORMATION

Strategies for handling conflict

The managing committee should try to identify potential areas of conflict or actual conflict early on. It should agree a process for handling the conflict.

1. **Identify the problem.**
   What is the conflict about? What is causing the conflict? Is there an underlying cause? Who is involved? What is the impact of the conflict?

2. **Explore the problem.**
   Discuss the problem with all parties involved. What are the different views on how it arose and how it might be resolved?

3. **Find solutions.**
   Look for solutions that will resolve the underlying causes as well as the immediate problem. If possible, find solutions which meet all or most of the needs of each party. These are described as **"win/win" solutions**. Try to avoid solutions which leave one party as the obvious loser. This may simply create more conflict.

An outsider may act as:

- **Facilitator:** enabling the people involved to sort out the problems.
- **Mediator:** helping all sides to resolve the problem.
- **Arbitrator:** gathering information and giving a judgement on what action should be taken.

If all this fails, one or another or the parties may decide to go to the law and seek litigation to resolve the dispute. The legal process should be seen as the very last resort.

If your organisation does decide to involve an outside person, make sure that you establish:

- A **contract** giving details of the work which will be done, how and with which people in the organisation.

CHECK POINT

Handling conflict

- Does your managing committee receive enough information to be able to identify potential conflict early?
- Who is responsible for dealing with conflict, should it arise?
- Does your organisation have agreed procedures for handling conflict?
- Do you know where to look for outside people or organisations that can help your organisation to deal with conflict?

- Who will **manage the contract**, on behalf of the organisation.
- The **results** you hope to see from the work.
- **Ground rules** for confidentiality, style of working, etc.

Try to avoid setting the outside consultant up as a magician who will wave a wand and solve all your problems. Remember – the conflict is your organisation's problem. A consultant can only enable your organisation to find solutions. She or he cannot impose solutions on you.

How to find a suitable outside consultant is covered later in this section.

Reviving a flagging organisation

Sometimes organisations get stuck doing the same old work in the same old way. You may be able to generate new energy and enthusiasm by taking time to reflect on fundamental questions such as:

- Are we really meeting the needs that we were set up to tackle?
- Have the needs changed? Why?
- Is our mission still relevant?
- Are the organisation's objectives clear and understood?
- What are our main achievements?

Example
The divided committee

The managing committee of a local arts organisation has split in to two warring camps. The split followed the election of three new, radical members to the committee. The new members tried to steer the organisation down a new path. Some existing members took umbrage. Personalities and styles clashed. The two sides began to make accusations each about the other. The new members claimed there were financial irregularities. Things slid downhill fast. Meetings became long, angry shouting matches. The staff in the organisation started to lose confidence in the committee. Staff were dragged into the conflict after accusations about staff performance were made.

The two major funders of the organisation who each had observers on the managing committee, both told the committee to sort itself out, or risk losing its funding. They suggested that a consultant be brought in to help to resolve the conflict.

Following a meeting with the whole committee, a consultant was appointed. She agreed to meet each person, in confidence. She wrote a report and discussed it with the whole committee.

Various further meetings took place to agree the best way forward and a plan of action. Eventually the committee agreed to a plan except for one person, who resigned, threatening legal action.

- Are we working as effectively as possible to achieve our objectives?
- What impact are we having?
- What needs to be done to take the organisation forward?

Your managing committee should set aside time each year to carry out this kind of review. It helps if the organisation already has clear forward plans and a strategy for achieving them.

From time to time, a more thorough review is needed. Very often this process is helped by involving someone from outside the organisation. It may be time to approach a consultant to help you. The consultant can work as a general facilitator of the review, or might be a specialist covering an area of particular concern to your organisation – such as organisational structure, or managing people.

Involving an outside consultant

We have mentioned that outside consultants can be useful to help organisations resolve conflict and to review progress. Consultants may also be valuable in the following ways:

- Bringing in skills and expertise not present in the organisation.
- Carrying out a project or specific piece of work which cannot be done by existing staff or volunteers.
- Bringing in new or different viewpoint or perspective.
- Helping an organisation solve problems.
- Helping to facilitate a process such as running a conference or large meeting.
- Helping the organisation to change and develop.

Your organisation should draw up a brief setting out exactly what you want the consultant to do, and the budget available, before you start looking for someone to do the work. The brief will enable you to identify what skills and experience the consultant must have. This will help you to select fairly.

Finding the consultant

There are three main ways to find a consultant:

- Use your organisation's existing networks to identify suitable people and consultancy organisations.
- Use databases of consultants such as

The consultancy brief

This should include:

- Description of your organisation and its purpose and values.
- The need for the consultancy - the problem the organisation is trying to solve.
- The outcomes that the organisation wants from the consultancy. These should be specific.
- An outline of how the work might be carried out.
- The budget and timescale.
- The skills and experience required in the consultants to do the work.

TECHNICAL DETAIL

those kept by the National Council for Voluntary Organisations or the Arts Council.

- Advertise publicly for a consultant.

Your organisation should invite the consultants to tender for the work as outlined in the brief. You will then need to meet selected consultants and choose which one best meets the requirements.

See that your organisation has clear criteria for selecting the consultants. These include:

- Skills and experience.
- Track record.
- References and recommendations.
- Cost.
- Availability to do the work when you need it done.

The cost of consultancy

Independent consultants may be freelance individuals or organisations. In general, consultants have to cover the whole of their operational costs from the contracts on which they work. Most charge by the day, some will give a costing for a completed piece of work. Good consultancy is not cheap. Don't make the mistake of immediately going

69

Involving a consultant

CHECK POINT

When using an outside consultant, does your organisation:

- Clearly identify the need for the consultant?

- Allocate an adequate budget for the work?

- Spell out the outcomes that are expected?

- Recruit the best consultant for the job?

- Agree a written contract?

- Plan how the organisation will use the results of the consultancy?

for the cheapest tender. It is more important to get consultants with the right skills and experience who can deliver what you want, in the way you want it. It is much more expensive to have to re-do the work of inadequate consultants who seemed cheap at the outset.

Managing the consultants

Once you have chosen a consultant and agreed a final contract, your organisation should make sure that it has adequate procedures for managing the work that will be done. This should not involve interference in the day to day work of the consultants but should establish a clear line of communication between the consultants and the organisation. Contractual details should normally be dealt with by a designated member of staff.

Many organisations set up a small Working Group to act as a "Think Tank" and point of reference for the consultancy. This group will also receive and discuss reports from the consultants.

The result of a consultancy

Most consultancies lead to a report recommending a course of action to the organisation. Your organisation will get

the best value from a consultancy if it builds in ways to discuss and implement the recommendations. These include:

- Meetings of staff and volunteers, service users, trustees to discuss the report.

- Meetings to plan action as a result of the report.

- Review of progress 3 or 6 months after the report.

Don't assume that a report on its own will necessarily lead to change.

For more on consultancy see *Books 20 and 21* in *Chapter 10*.

Self-assessment

Dealing with problems

		Know	Must check
1.	What should organisations do to avoid crises?	☐	☐
2.	What causes conflict in organisations?	☐	☐
3.	What are the three main stages in handling conflict?	☐	☐
4.	What are three sensible ground rules for resolving conflict?	☐	☐
5.	What are the advantages of using an outside person or organisation to help resolve a conflict?	☐	☐
6.	What are five of the ways in which a consultant can help an organisation?	☐	☐
7.	What should be included in a consultancy brief?	☐	☐
8.	What are the three main ways to find a consultant?	☐	☐
9.	How can an organisation make sure that a consultancy doesn't just end with a report?	☐	☐

Getting the most from being a trustee

You have no formal obligation to get the most from being a trustee! You are allowed to be as miserable as you like! However, most people will want to enjoy and make the most of their work as a trustee. The committee itself should make sure that it provides sufficient back up and support to each of its members, so that they are all satisfied and able to enjoy the work.

1. Know what is expected of you

Make sure you fully understand what being a member of the managing committee involves.

See that you are provided with proper information about being a trustee and proper induction.

Check that you have sufficient time to carry out the job. There is nothing worse than agreeing to do something that you know you will not be able to do properly.

2. Don't worry unnecessarily about your liabilities

Take your role seriously but don't lie awake at night worrying about possible personal liabilities. Remember that the law provides considerable protection for you provided that you have behaved honestly and taken reasonable care in carrying out your duties.

3. Get to know the other trustees

Try to build up a good working knowledge of the skills and experience that the other members of the committee bring to the work.

Aim to establish trust and rapport with your co-trustees. Don't expect to do this overnight. Trustees meet infrequently, so it takes time for new members to feel part of the team.

If possible, time should be set aside for trustees to meet less formally, outside the committee meetings. Some ideas are given in *Chapter 2*.

4. Keep informed about the work of your organisation

Make sure you are in touch with what is going on. The committee exists to enable your organisation to do its work well. Part of your reward for being a committee member is knowing that the work is being done well.

If you can, visit the organisation regularly to see what is going on and meet the staff and volunteers. This will help you to keep a clear idea of the needs the organisation is trying to meet, and how it is going about it. It will help you to keep the values and spirit of your organisation alive.

5. If in doubt always ask

As a trustee you must be properly informed. If you are unclear about what is going on or don't understand something, always ask.

Encourage a culture in which trustees are expected to ask questions.

6. Know where to go for information and advice

Use your own organisation – another committee member or a volunteer may know the answer.

If not, approach your organisation's legal or financial advisers for help.

If you still need information contact one of the organisations listed in *Chapter 10*. They will either answer your question or direct you to an organisation which can.

7. Don't get overloaded with details

Your main task is to keep a clear overview of the affairs of your organisation. Don't get bogged down in day-to-day details. Delegate these to sub-committees and to staff.

Try to keep your papers in reasonable order. You may find it helpful to use the *"Trustee Organiser"* produced by the Directory of Social Change. (*Book 22 in Chapter 10*).

8. Involve yourself in appropriate sub-committees

Give time, if you can, to sub-committees or working groups. Focus your efforts on those that interest you and which make use your particular skills and experience. This work will make you more aware of the organisation's work and will bring you more informal contact with other committee members and staff.

9. Allocate time between meetings for preparation and follow up

Set aside time in your diary for reading the minutes and committee papers before meetings. Don't leave everything to the last minute.

Keep a record of decisions which require you to do something. Don't wait for the minutes to arrive before you do anything. Plan what you will do and when you will do it immediately after the meeting. Allocate time to do it, in your diary.

10. Set priorities for your work

You know what your main interests and skills are. Give priority to work on the committee or in sub-committees that makes best use of them. Don't unquestioningly agree to undertake more and more work. Know the limits to your time. Be prepared to say "no".

11. Attend committee meetings

It may seem glaringly obvious that managing committee members should make every effort to attend the meetings. Try never to be absent without good reason. Remember you are responsible for all decisions taken by the committee, whether or not you were part of the meeting.

12. Attend the Annual General Meeting

Make sure you attend the AGM. This is a most important meeting.

13. Review your work as a committee member

Find time to pause and ask yourself whether you are doing a good job? Are you still enjoying the work? If not, why? Is it time to change or move on?

14. Reclaim any out-of-pocket expenses

You give your time for free to the organisation. You should not be expected also to bear out of pocket costs that you incur.

The committee should make sure that the organisation has clear, simple and quick systems for repaying the out-of-pocket expenses of committee members.

15. Pat yourself on the back occasionally

Finally, don't forget that your work is voluntary. This means you have chosen to do it. Take a few moments from time to time to reflect on why you are prepared to give up your leisure time to sit on the committee and undertake the work that this involves? Why is this important to you? Why do you do it?

Recognise the importance of the work you do. You are helping your organisation to do something worthwhile which makes a real difference to the lives of the people or whatever else benefits from its work, or the wider community it serves.

Your work as a trustee matters. It makes a difference. Enjoy it!

Five ways to get more from being a trustee

ACTIVITY

1 Think carefully why you want to do the job.

It is a voluntary commitment. You do it because you want to, not because you have to. Are you committed to the cause, the values and the ethos of the organisation? Do you want to influence it or change it?

2 Make a list of what you want out of the job.

Use the list below to identify the main things you want from you trusteeship.

A sense of achievement from helping the organisation to achieve its goals.

Power and influence.

Being part of an effective team with your co-trustees.

Contacts with the other trustees.

The chance to specialise in an area of the work in which you have particular competence or interest.

Good working relationships with staff.

Access to training and support.

Access to good information.

Access to conferences.

Social contacts.

Networking and contact with other organisations.

Developing your committee skills.

Feedback on your performance on the committee.

Recognition of your particular expertise or experience.

Using your skills to benefit the organisation or its work.

A sense of fulfilment.

Seeing the results of the organisation's work through field-visits, etc.

Attending seminars and presentations on the work of the organisation.

Having fun and enjoyment.

Others *(add your own)*:

3 Make a list of what you bring to the work.

- Your skills.   .
- Your experience.
- Your time.
- Your perspective.
- Others *(add your own)*:

How can you use these attributes most effectively on the committee?

4 Check to see that there is a balance between what you contribute and what you get in return.

5 Review your work regularly.

Is it a source of delight to you? Do you enjoy it? Would you much rather be spending a rainy winter's evening in Scunthorpe? Is it time to revive your commitment or to retire and make way for someone else?

Resources

BOOKLIST

Useful publications

The books listed below are available from the publisher, unless otherwise stated. The publisher's address is also listed or is given in the list of useful addresses which follows.

Making meetings effective

Book 1. **Just about managing? Effective management for voluntary organisations and community groups.** Sandy Adirondack. 1992. London Voluntary Service Council, 68 Chalton Street, London, NW1 1JR. £10.95.

Book 2. **Planning together: the art of effective teamwork.** George Gawlinski and Lois Graessle. Bedford Square Press. 1988. From the National Council for Voluntary Organisations, Regent's Wharf, 8 All Saints Street, London, N1 9RL. £11.95.

Book 3. **How to make meetings work.** Malcolm Peel. 1988. Kogan Page. From bookshops. £5.95.

Book 4. **Seeing it through: how to be effective on a committee.** Steve Clarke. Community Development Foundation/Bedford Square Press 1992. From National Council for Voluntary Organisations. £3.95.

Book 5. **Improving work groups: a practical manual for team building.** Dave Francis and Don Young. University Associates. 1979 (Revised 1993). Pfeiffer and Company, 862, Garrett Lane, London, SW17 0NB. £34.95

Managing people

Book 6. **Voluntary not amateur: a guide to the law for voluntary organisations and community groups.** Duncan Forbes, Ruth Hayes and Jacki Reason. London Voluntary Service Council. 1990. £7.95 from Directory of Social Change.

Book 7. **How to make your management style more effective.** W.J. Reddin. McGraw Hill. 1987. From bookshops.

Book 8. **Helping people work together: a guide to participative working practices.** Robin Douglas et al. 1988. National Institute for Social Work Paper No. 21. £6.00

Book 9. **The Inland Revenue** provides free explanatory leaflets:

P7	Employers Guide to Pay As You Earn
IR53	Thinking of taking someone on? PAYE for Employers

Book 10. **ACAS** (The Advisory, Conciliation and Arbitration Service) provides free explanatory leaflets. From ACAS, Clifton House, 83-117, Euston Road, London NW1 2RB 071 388 5100:

Discipline at work

Employing people - Handbook for small firms

Itemised pay statement

Book 11. **The Department of Employment provides free leaflets** (available from Job Centres):

PL700   Written statement of main terms and conditions of employment

PL710   Employment rights for the expectant mother

PL833   Redundancy: consultation and notification

PL808   Redundancy payments.

Caxton House, Tothill Street, London SW1H 9NF 071 273 3000

Book 12. **The Department of Social Security (DSS) provides free leaflets.** For example:

NI 268 Quick Guide to National Insurance, Statutory Sick Pay and Statutory Maternity Pay.

Alexander Fleming House, Newington Causeway, London SE1 6BY 071 407 5522

Book 13. **A guide to performance appraisal.** Alan Rogers. 1987. Council for Education and Training in Youth and Community Work, Wellington House, Wellington Street, Leicester. £3.00.

Managing volunteers

Book 14. **Volunteers first: the personnel responsibilities of people who manage volunteers.** Angie McDonough and Angela Whitcher. 1991. Volunteer Centre UK. 29, Lower King's Road, Berkhamsted, Herts. HP4 2AB

Book 15. **Managing volunteers - a handbook for volunteer organisers.** 1992. Volunteer Centre UK.

Book 16. **Managing volunteers.** Elaine Willis. In *"Issues in Voluntary and Non-profit Management"*. Edited by Julian Batsleer, Chris Cornforth and Rob Paton. Open University reader. 1992. Addison Wesley. From bookshops or the publisher.

Recruitment

Book 17. **Fair interviewing**. 1992 Annie Hedge and Barbara Darling. Trentham Books. From bookshops. £8.95. Very clear guidance on how to interview fairly.

Running premises

Book 18. **Managing your community building** 1993. Peter Hudson. Community Matters. 8-9 Upper Street, London, N1 0PQ. £13.95

Book 19. **Finding and running premises: a guide for voluntary organisations.** 1985. Judith Unell and Anne Weyman. Bedford Square Press/NCVO.

Dealing with problems

Book 20. **Making the best use of consultants 1992.** Philip Hope. Longman UK. From bookshops. £19.95

Book 21. **Managing consultancy: a Guide for arts and voluntary organisations.** 1990. National Council for Voluntary Organisations and the Arts Council of Great Britain.

Better trusteeship

Book 22. **The trustee organiser.** 1993. Directory of Social Change. £12.50. An invaluable pack that provides information and a structure in which you can insert all the relevant details of your organisation.

Book 23. **How to be a better trustee.** Part One: Roles and Responsibilities. Kevin Ford. 1993. Directory of Social Change. Part Two: Aims, Accountability and Resources; Part Three: People, Premises and problems. £35 each part; £95 for the complete set. Self-contained training and learning materials on trusteeship for use by trainers, organisations and trustees themselves.

Book 24. **The good trustee guide.** 1994. National Council for Voluntary Organisations. £8.95. A loose leaf binder packed with information on a wide range of matters which a trustee is responsible for.

Book 25. **Training for trustees.** A regular newsletter produced by the Trustee Services Unit of the National Council for Voluntary Organisations, Regents Wharf, 8 All Saints Street, London N1 9RL.

Other information

The Charity Commission provide advice and information to charities. Northern Office, Graeme House, Derby Square, Liverpool L2 7SB; or Central Register, St Alban's House, 57/60 Haymarket, London SW1Y 4QX.

The Charity Commission has a number of telephone advice lines on the 1992 and 1993 Charities Acts. It also provides a free video on the role and responsibilities of trustees.

The National Council for Voluntary Organisations provides information and advice on trusteeship through its Trustee Services Unit. Regent's Wharf, 8 All Saints Street, London N1 9RL.

The Trustee Services Unit runs a free **Trustee Information and Advice Line** for trustees. **071-833 1818.**

ACAS (The Advisory, Conciliation and Arbitration Service) provides advice and help with problems such as disciplinary procedure, industrial relations resolution of conflict and related staffing issues. ACAS, Clifton House, 83-117, Euston Road, London NW1 2RB 071-388 5100.

The Trustee Register, 114 Peascod Street, Windsor, Berkshire SL4 1DN keeps a register of people who want to be charity trustees. It offers a free service to organisations looking for new trustees.

Information and advice on all aspects of voluntary work can be obtained from

The Volunteer Centre UK, 29 Lower King's Road, Berkhamsted, Herts HP4 2AB.

Similar information and advice can be obtained locally from your nearest **Volunteer Bureau**. For details of the location of volunteer bureaux contact the National Association of Volunteer Bureaux, St.Peter's College, College Road, Saltley, Birmingham B8 3TE.

The law affecting charities is different in Northern Ireland and Scotland. For more information contact:

- **Northern Ireland Council for Voluntary Action**, 127 Ormeau Road, Belfast BT7 1SH.

- **Northern Ireland Charities Unit,** Department of Finance and Personnel, Room 255, Parliament Buildings, Stormont, Belfast BT4 3SW.

- **Scottish Council for Community and Voluntary Organisations,** 19 Claremont Crescent, Edinburgh EH7 4QD.

If you are a local organisation, you should first approach your nearest **Council for Voluntary Service** or **Rural Community Council** (England), **County Voluntary Council** (Wales) or **Council for Social Service** (Scotland). These organisations should be able to provide you with initial help and advice, and point you towards other sources of information.

Index